What People Are Saying...

Many thanks for a great book. I will also share it with some of my colleagues who teach leadership. Keep in touch, and I look forward to meeting you in future workshops on RU campus.

Dr. Lei Lei, Professor
Chair, Department of SCM & Marketing Sciences
Director, Rutgers Center for SCM
Rutgers Business School, Rutgers University

★★★★★ *Decisive Leadership*: Help for Us All! *Decisive Leadership* is a great read: realistic, straightforward, and fast-paced! For all of us who lose our balance on a daily basis, it provides a touch stone to keep us on our feet and moving forward in a positive direction... Anthony Jackson has a winner here!

Dale Dvorak
CEO, Medicia Holdings

★★★★★ Practical leadership practices in a complex environment are a tough commodity to find. Mr. Jackson has been able to meld personal experience and old world philosophy into a reference handbook for all of us in these difficult times. The times call for everyone in all organizations to understand and be accountable for unlocking their leadership skills. We can all see ourselves in the cases presented and this time gain some insights on how to approach these challenges in the future. Read it on the train and/or give it to your Teams - it's time to take the first step.

Len DeCandia
Chief Procurement Officer, Estée Lauder

★★★★★ Valuable life lessons whether you are in the corporate world or not, this book offers valuable life lessons to all of us. The character of Kelsey Knowles brings clarity to situations with such ease, you are left saying "why didn't I see it that way?" Self-evaluation sometimes needs self-assurance to do so, and Kelsey offers that assistance in this book. I can't wait to see what lives he changes next!

Lori Nickerson
President & CEO, HMC Dental Handpiece Repair

★★★★★ I had the opportunity to read the book this weekend, and I wanted to pass along my positive reaction to it. I finished it in one setting, and I enjoyed it very much. Lots to learn about change and about trying to get the value from consultants and outside perspectives. You should be very proud of this work and the legacy you leave with it. *Decisive Leadership* is a great story about change management in a corporate culture. There are some very valuable lessons about listening, supporting others, and influencing change. As a 25 year career corporate professional, I sincerely valued the lessons and would encourage all to read.

George Harry
Director, Global Transportation Organization
Johnson & Johnson Sales & Logistics Company, LLC

Prof. Lei and I will certainly enjoy reading our signed copies of *Decisive Leadership*! I read the first two chapters over the weekend and I really like the way the characters' stories are weaved together throughout the chapters. I'm looking forward to finishing the book.

Corinne Schiavo
Sr. Business Administrator
Rutgers Center for Supply Chain Management

★★★★★ A fabulous and quick read. I particularly love the style of this book. It is not about theory or concepts. The book reflects the real world and real circumstances to give you the message in context. Not like your standard leadership books. This book uses a real life dialogue of various people to demonstrate common situations we find ourselves in. It then shows how they are lead to getting focus in not just work, but also their personal lives, which in the end leads to greater outcomes in all areas of their lives. A lot of "Ah-ha" moments while you read this book. Each page there is something you can learn and apply to your life!

Jennifer M. Swayze
Project Manager, Global Recruiting
University Specialty Group at Johnson & Johnson

★★★★★ Great and relevant book! Anthony T. Jackson's book, *Decisive Leadership* is a great book, because it is filled with real situations. I saw myself and recognized people (types) that I work with. The main message is to achieve balance in your life, personal/professional. Mr. Jackson claims that you really can not separate the two. And he is right. This book can start you down the road to having a more balanced focused approach to solving the problems we face in corporate America. I highly recommend getting and reading this book.

A. R. Burke
Engineer, Lockheed Martin

★★★★★ Anthony Jackson's *Decisive Leadership* takes you along on a journey of self discovery through the characters in his book. This provides you with the ability to view situations through the eyes of others which is an extremely effective way to gain insight and perspective on how to deal with business and personal situations. Mr. Jackson gives us a multitude of relatable examples to which anyone can identify, by doing so he is able to reach a much larger audience.

Decisive Leadership: The Vision to See Beyond is an excellent learning tool for the individual as well as for seminar training. It provides you with the power to bring your workforce to its full potential by focusing on professional priorities as well as touching on the personal.

Kimberly McMullen
CPA, NJ State Department of Treasurer

Decisive Leadership reminds the reader that we are all human, with limitless potential so long as we retain clarity of thought. The cast of characters are relatable and attractive. The story reads like a soap opera - jumping from one character's corporate challenge, to the next personal struggle. This is a wonderful read. My only complaint is that it ended too soon.

Larysa S. Cohen
Performance and Process Manager, Roche Diagnostics

★★★★★ Living your life to the fullest to achieve professional and personal success! *Decisive Leadership* by Anthony Jackson is an easy quick read that inspires and promotes professional and personal success (as it may be fame, prosperity, or finding a companion for life — to name a few) and serves as a guide to achieving the desired outcomes in one's life, as they may be short or long term goals.

Decisive Leadership has been a daily reminder to me that by having physical, mental, and emotional balance and harmony, I would be sure to achieve inner peace and happiness, thus, live life to the fullest. When one is living to the fullest and free oneself from limitations, success is inevitable.

Katherine B. Han
Asst. Vice-President, American International Group

DECISIVE LEADERSHIP

– The Vision to See Beyond –

Decisive Leadership

Published by:
LEGACY PUBLISHING SERVICES
1883 Lee Road
Winter Park, Florida 32789
www.LegacyPublishing.org

Printed in the United States
ISBN: 978-1-934449-41-7

DECISIVE LEADERSHIP

– The Vision to See Beyond –

How One Person Can Save Your Corporation In Tough Economic Times

ANTHONY T. JACKSON

Another Quality Book Published By:
LEGACY PUBLISHING SERVICES
1883 Lee Road, Winter Park, FL 32789
WWW.LEGACYPUBLISHING.ORG

DEDICATION

To my loving wife and wonderful son,
who have inspired me to be more, do more,
and want more out of life.

ACKNOWLEDGEMENTS

How do you acknowledge all the people who have influenced your life? In creating "Decisive Leadership" there have been a few individuals that have contributed directly to this work. There are three individuals however, that have been instrumental in shaping how I view the world.

I will start by recognizing my great uncle, Eugene Coleman, who has been my father and my first mentor. Through his influence my character was forged into the person I am today.

My second mentor is Lt. Gen. Lloyd J. Austin III. At the time of publishing, LTG Austin's military role has him in Iraq as the Commanding General of Multi-National Corps-Iraq. He was my Tactical officer at West Point and my Battalion Executive officer at Fort Drum, NY where I led a Platoon of 30 Infantry Soldiers while attached to the B Co 2/22 Battalion, 1st Brigade, 10th Mountain Division. General Austin demonstrated through his actions what it means to truly lead and care about your soldiers.

My third and final mentor is Leonardo DeCandia. I have worked with him for almost half of my civilian career. Len has shown me the value of integrity and ethics in "Corporate America" and how the lack of those traits has led to the problems "Corporate America" is currently experiencing. Len created an environment that allowed me to grow under his tutelage, effectively creating a leadership style based on military values and sound corporate principles.

Other individuals that have helped shape the principles that are in "Decisive Leadership" are: Sifu

Louis Diaz, my Tai Chi instructor. His teachings have helped me achieve a balanced approach to life. By incorporating Tai Chi into my business & personal life, I finally understood the concept that Len was trying to teach me, "People and Corporations do not change, you have to change." I finally realized that the grass is not greener on the other side. It is how you deal with the problems that will determine success or failure.

Darren Johnson, a retired Army Sergeant, introduced me to Sifu about 9 years ago. Darren has become a very close friend & confidant, who is a great sounding board for some of my radical ideals.

Last, but not least, I would like to acknowledge Troy Rackley, who gave me my first corporate job out of the military. Troy's favorite saying was "Catch the wave or drown." We accomplished some pretty incredible things while I was at Nestle.

And to all my teachers, friends, and business associates who helped shape my thoughts and philosophies, thank you.

INTRODUCTION

Decisive Leadership is about one's journey of self-discovery and the courage necessary to implement change. It focuses on the following factors:

1. The ability to obtain mental clarity in order to see the decision that need to be made and more importantly the impact that those decisions will have on an organization.
2. Once you understand the decision that needs to be made, do you now have the courage to execute on those decisions and take the necessary personal risk to succeed or fail? Notice I said fail also. If you think you will always succeed then don't bother to read any further because you are living in a fantasy.

This book will explore the avenues to self-discovery utilizing concepts from Tai Chi & mediation techniques that allow for mental clarity that will then prepare you to execute against "Decisive Leadership" technique.

Properly executed as the title suggests, "one person can save your corporation". Although this is a fictional work, it is designed to allow one to instantly identify with a character. Through reading "Decisive Leadership", it is hoped that you will be able to transfer some of their lessons learned and apply them in your everyday situations. I hope you enjoy the collaboration of my brother, Frank E. Jackson, Jr., who helped to bring the characters to life and business insight I infused to create a fast-paced realistic story.

Jody Myers, a dear friend, and my wife Judy Jackson were also instrumental in helping to edit this work for your reading pleasure.

CHAPTER 1

As Konrad Jankowski awoke that morning, he slowly gazed at his surroundings. He wondered where the hell he was. Then he realized he'd fallen asleep in his office, the closest place to the bar where he had been intoxicated last night. He remembered having the wherewithal to stumble back to his office and not drive home.

Konrad was the CEO of Reality Solutions, Inc., a private labeling firm. His company's numbers were steadily dwindling for the last five quarters, and he could not seem to get a handle on the problem. Konrad was now spending five nights a week in bars instead of his customary two nights a week.

Konrad glanced at the photo of his mother and father as he pulled a bottle of Scotch from his desk drawer. He briefly reflected on his life back in Poland as a child. He remembered the poverty and the nights his father came home drunk and belligerent, disrupting the false happiness his mother attempted to provide for him and his brother.

Konrad downed the glass of Scotch.

He glanced at his parents' picture again as he prepared to pour another glass. He hesitated as he remembered the vow he made to himself the night his father struck his mother: never to become an alcoholic. But now, he was somehow able to relate to his father, who had eventually committed suicide after an endless bout with alcoholism and depression.

In years past, the resentment and animosity Konrad harbored as a result of his father's addiction prevented any level of empathy for his father's legacy. Yet as he pondered the fate of Reality Solutions, Inc. and his own financial future, he wondered about the circumstances that could have led his father to such extremes. How had Konrad lost control? How had he lost sight of that which really mattered? At what point had his business decisions and instincts failed him? Had he allowed the influence of Wall Street analysts and soaring stock prices to dictate the direction of his company?

Konrad could not believe he was contemplating quitting his company, just throwing in the towel. As he prepared to pour himself another drink, the phone rang. He was so startled that he dropped the bottle. The Scotch sloshed over the desk and dripped onto his shirt, triggering a string of curses. Few people knew that Konrad would at times be at his desk at 6:00 a.m. After a moment of ignoring the phone, curiosity finally overcame his reluctance and he answered the phone.

"Konrad Jankowski speaking."

"Mr. Jankowski?"

"Speaking."

"Kelsey Knowles here."

Konrad paused after he heard the name. Where had he heard the name before? Kelsey sensed Konrad's thoughts.

"Kelsey Knowles, the author of *Decisive Leadership*."

"Oh! Kelsey Knowles! My apologies, it's been so long. When was the last time we spoke?"

"Actually, this is the first time. You left me a message two weeks ago. I've just returned from a promotional tour, and now I'm catching up on all my phone calls."

"Well, it's a pleasure to finally speak with you. After reading your book, I knew I had to meet you."

"Are you available today?"

Konrad hesitated at Kelsey's abruptness. Calling before 7:00 a.m.? Wanting to meet on the same day? It seemed a bit rushed. Regardless, his curiosity prevailed.

"Sure. I don't have any lunch plans," he replied while reviewing his calendar and scratching out his original lunch plans.

"Great! I'll see you at noon, at your office."

Konrad put the bottle away and cleaned up the spill. He was in deep thought as he pulled out a new shirt from a stack he kept in his office. His thirst had just been replaced by an overwhelming feeling of anticipation. Maybe today was the day he'd been waiting for. Maybe today he would get some of the answers he had been looking for.

Kelsey smiled as he replaced the receiver. He was often amused by how his abruptness could cause such uneasiness in others. He reflected on the days when he was bound by society's unspoken rules: Never make a business call before 8:00 a.m.; no personal calls before noon on weekends; never appear too anxious. The list seemed endless. He was just happy to be free.

Kelsey had just completed his Tai Chi workout, a vital part of his morning routine. It was now as natural to him as brushing his teeth.

Western societies dictate basic steps for a prosperous and acceptable life: Obtain a degree, and subsequently a good job. Kelsey had complied. Though he leaned toward a military career in high school, he kept his options open by taking the usual college preparatory classes, participating in student government activities and in sports, especially in football, where he excelled. His talent in football garnered him significant interest from Vanderbilt University which eventually offered him an athletic scholarship. However, the scholarship was contingent upon his not sustaining any injuries during his collegiate football career.

Kelsey was seriously considering an academic career at Vanderbilt until his Advanced English class invited a cadet from the United States Military Academy at West Point to speak. The cadet explained the advantages of a full scholarship. Kelsey knew then that going to West Point was the way to fulfill his dreams. After graduating from West Point and serving his country for eight years, including the first Gulf War and the Somalia Conflict, he decided to leave the military and join corporate America. He started as a supervisor in a Fortune 500 company working on the manufacturing floor; and after a series of successful business decisions over the next 10 years, he became a Vice President in the pharmaceutical industry. By the age of 36, he had risen to the level of corporate executive, but he had forgotten about one important factor during his drive to succeed and become Mr. Corporate—himself.

Stress began to eat away at Kelsey's entire being like a cancer. He had gained 50 extra pounds and was wearing the face of a stress-riddled, prematurely aging man. His personal relationship had failed after it crumbled to nothing recognizable. His situation continued to worsen until he did the unthinkable. He quit his job. No warning. No thought. He just quit. He took his savings and spent the next six months traveling in other countries. It was during this time that he began to reflect on his life experiences, in and away from constantly climbing the corporate ladder. He realized the decline of his health and other endeavors should never have reached such a level of unmanageability, and he was determined to figure out how it happened. After putting things in proper perspective, he wanted to share his discovery of oneself and experiences with others who desperately needed his help. The result was his novel, *Decisive Leadership.*

Kelsey glanced up at the wall where the first printed copy of his book hung, framed in a glass case. Because of the success of his book, he was bombarded with requests from all types of organizations to conduct seminars and give keynote speeches.

Out of the 15 messages he had listened to the night before, Konrad Jankowski's was the first Kelsey returned. Of all the requests, Konrad's call seemed a genuine and urgent call for help. Many of the other voices were those who would praise him as long as the media did. He would get to them later.

****

Susan Lockhart's hand reluctantly appeared from beneath her blanket to turn off the alarm. She was irritated. The alarm had pulled her from a heartwarming dream. She had just spent all day with her sweetheart. Her irritation turned into disappointment as she realized it was just a dream. She sat up in bed and stared at herself through the mirror on her dresser. As she ran her hand through her shoulder-length blond hair, she wondered why she didn't have a boyfriend. She was attractive. She could feel the stares of her admirers as she strode purposefully down the streets of Washington, DC in her form-fitting business suits, but no one would approach her. Those who did were not intellectually stimulating.

Susan, a 31 year-old who looked as though she were in her twenties, was at the top of her game. She graduated top of her class from George Washington University where she majored in accounting. She had changed companies three times since her graduation. Each change represented a significant jump in salary and responsibility. Her current position was with Reality Solutions, Inc. The owner, Konrad Jankowski, was impressed with her assertiveness and felt she could play a vital role in turning his Accounting Department around. Susan jumped at the opportunity. It was her first department head position, and she knew it would allow her an opportunity to implement her own strategies versus just following orders. It didn't hurt that she felt she would really like working for Konrad. Maybe it was because of his age, but she felt she wouldn't have to play the typical corporate games around him; his major concern was results. She hoped that in this new role, her superiors and peers would respect her for what she knew and not how she looked. Time would tell.

****

Konrad was reviewing his task list for the day when he heard a knock at his door.

"Konrad?"

He sighed as he recognized the voice, Edward Starks, his COO. Konrad couldn't put his finger on it; but for the last year or so, Edward's very presence just plain irritated him. But he couldn't bring himself to deal with his feelings because Edward had been with him from the beginning. Only five years his junior at 55 years old, Edward had played an integral part in planning the IPO that took Reality Solutions, Inc. public.

"Come in, Edward."

"Good morning," Edward said as he closed the door. "Are we still on for lunch today?"

"Actually, something has come up."

"Oh, really?"

"Yes, I'll be meeting with Kelsey Knowles today," said Konrad, "the author of *Decisive Leadership.*"

"I know who he is," said Edward. "Are you thinking about having him conduct a seminar or speech or something?"

Konrad paused, sensing the anticipation in Edward's voice. He didn't like how easily Edward was threatened by others.

"I have not decided on that yet," said Konrad.

Edward was brusque. "Well, he's probably busy anyway. I never have been crazy about those consultants turned authors who write books on subjects that it's taken others years to perfect, just to make a quick buck. You know what I mean?"

"Perhaps. But we're obviously doing something wrong. Maybe he'll have a few ideas. It certainly can't hurt just to listen."

"That was actually one of the things that I wanted to discuss with you today at lunch. I've received complaints regarding two of our new department heads."

"Who?"

"Susan Lockhart and Joshua Brown."

Konrad knew that Edward wasn't excited about the new hires anyhow so he wasn't surprised when he heard those two names. He wondered about the true origin of the complaints, and decided to dismiss the issue until later.

"I have some thoughts I want to share with you," Edward persisted.

"That sounds good, Edward. Let's get together some time after lunch."

Konrad simply wasn't in the mood. He was excited about his lunch appointment. He didn't want to allow anything to damper his optimism, to jeopardize his chance for a better path.

****

Joshua Brown stared out the window daydreaming as his metro train emerged from underground onto a bridge that crossed the Potomac River connecting Washington, DC and Arlington, Virginia. He was proud of himself. He had graduated from Howard University with a business degree and was now the Director of Operations for Reality Solutions, Inc.

He was happy that he had somehow evaded the fate that fell upon so many of his family and peers. His older brother was killed at the age of 16 in a drive-by shooting while playing stickball on a corner. Joshua was 12 years old when it happened. Now he was 35 years old, running a department of 50 employees and working for a company once considered the fastest growing private labeling company in America.

Joshua was accustomed to working hard and dealing with difficult tasks. He considered himself a "firefighting expert" in solving business issues, which is why he considered Reality Solutions the perfect place to be.

Joshua was determined to prove himself in his first Director position. He knew it would take hard work and commitment to be successful. Hard work was never a problem for him. During his teenage years, while his friends were playing games in the summer, he went door to door with a lawn mower setting up yard work contracts for the summer months. He learned at an early age that there is no substitute for hard work. Now here he was facing his largest challenge thus far, and he was determined to be successful. Failure was not an option.

****

"Mr. Jankowski, Mr. Kelsey Knowles is here to see you," announced the receptionist through Konrad's speaker phone.

"Thank you. Send him in."

Konrad was nervous as he adjusted his tie. He wondered why he was so jittery. He considered that he was about to have lunch with a famous writer, but that wasn't the true reason. There was something deeper, but his initial reason would have to suffice for now.

"Mr. Knowles," Konrad said extending his hand as Kelsey entered.

"Mr. Jankowski, it's my pleasure."

Konrad was startled at Kelsey's demeanor. Suddenly the everyday phrase "it's my pleasure" took on an entire new meaning after Kelsey said it. It actually seemed as though he meant it.

"Mine as well. Please, have a seat."

"Thank you."

"Do you have a restaurant preference, Mr. Knowles?"

"Please call me Kelsey."

"Kelsey it is. So where do you—"

"Sam's Cafe"

"Sam's Cafe?"

"Yep, I haven't eaten there in ages, and they're renowned for their turkey club."

"Really? I had this really nice restaurant in mind. Are you sure that's all you want?"

Kelsey remembered the time when he would have succumbed to the typical exclusive meal at a prestigious restaurant, but that time was no more.

"Yes, I'm sure. I've followed a strict diet for the past two months, and I'm ready to break it."

Konrad wondered if this was some sort of trick.

Kelsey decided they would go to the Arlington location of Sam's café and Konrad realized he didn't know how to get there.

"Don't worry," Kelsey assured. "I'll drive."

This wasn't working out quite the way Konrad expected. Here he was on the passenger side of a two-door, Honda Insight Hybrid, on his way to Sam's Cafe with a consultant he was seriously considering to help turn his company around. He had expected to be chauffeuring Kelsey in his Mercedes-Benz on their way to a prestigious restaurant on Capitol Hill. In fact, initially Konrad was downright irritated. Heading to a sandwich shop as a passenger in an economy car was completely out of his style, but for some reason he succumbed to this silent power which emanated from Kelsey. To further complicate matters, Kelsey was playing music that Konrad only heard on television infomercials advertising Yoga workout videos. But as strange as everything seemed, Konrad couldn't resist. In fact, to his surprise, he found himself starting to relax and feel comfortable—or better yet, safe.

****

Kelsey briefly pondered how his meeting with Konrad would turn out, how he could influence the conversation to ensure a contracted engagement. But that train of thought didn't last long. Kelsey quickly remembered it did not pay to force a solution. He learned long ago the dangers of forcing an environment to his will. Once the desired result was obtained, the benefits quickly vanished once he left. Why? Because the external pressure was no longer present.

In the past, Kelsey's external pressure was his force of will to be successful. In forcing his will, he knew he could bring change, but he also knew forced change could not be sustained. He had to first enroll people in his vision, and then prepare the environment to absorb and continually facilitate the change. Without a shared vision, people and processes would always return to a comfort zone, even if old ways jeopardized business.

Kelsey understood that sustainable change was also contingent upon a self-reliant team. Teams that are unable to function during interruptions of leadership will ultimately cripple an organization. Kelsey knew he would have to help people in a way that enabled them to be self-empowered to sustain themselves once he left.

Kelsey's experiences had taught him to relax and allow things to progress at a natural, sustainable pace with just enough stimuli to keep things rolling. Change must balance the speed of culture with the discomfort inherent to breaking a new path. Through his Tai Chi training, Kelsey learned that the answer to his problems sourced within. Through harmonization of mental, physical and spiritual health, answer resided just below the surface of thought, within the subconscious. The more one relaxed, the easier it was for "the" answer to surface. It had taken him some time to grasp this concept, but his Sifu, who had trained in China and who captained the U.S.A. Wushu Team, eventually succeeded in explaining to him that this is a naturally occurring phenomenon in all of us.

Sifu explained that Tai Chi, as it is practiced in the West today, can perhaps best be thought of as a moving form of yoga and meditation combined. Many of these movements originally derived from the martial arts, which in turn derived from the natural movements of animals and birds. Movements are performed in Tai Chi slowly, softly, and gracefully with smooth and even transitions in between.

For many practitioners, the focus in Tai Chi movement is not first and foremost martial, but rather a meditative exercise for the body. For others, the combat aspects of Tai Chi are of considerable interest.

Another aim of Tai Chi is to foster a calm and tranquil mind focused on the precise execution of these exercises. Learning the exercises correctly provides a practical avenue for learning about balance and alignment. Furthermore, the meditative nature of the exercises is calming and relaxing in and of itself.

Something his Sifu had told him resurfaced in his mind: "Kelsey, think back to when you had a difficult problem and for the life of you, you could not solve it. Finally, when you were exhausted and closed your eyes to sleep, something marvelous happened. You awoke in an epiphany. You now had the solution that had long eluded you. Think back to a time when you were driving home from work and you let the music take you to another place, and how easy it was for those solutions to reveal themselves. There is no answer that you do not already know. What I will teach you is to actively learn how to access your subconscious and to

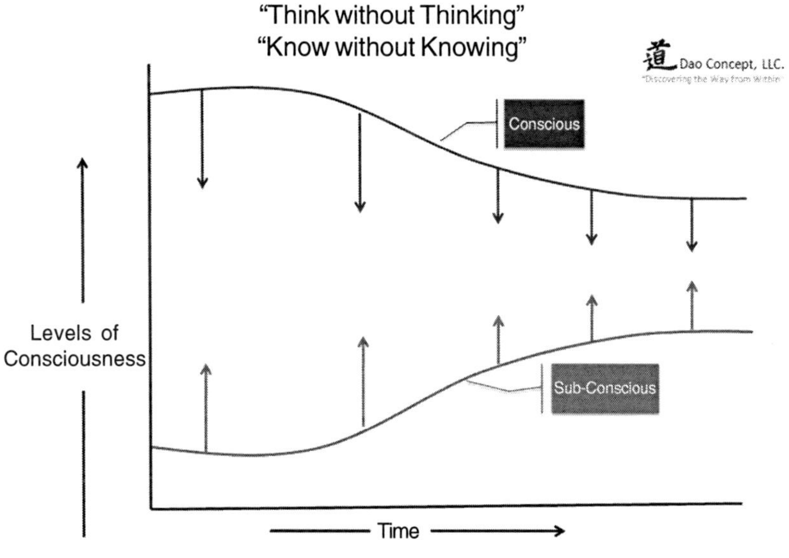

"The measure of success is not whether you have a tough problem to deal with, but whether it is the same problem you had last year"

- John Foster Dulles

find the solutions that already exist; this is called the universal knowledge source."

Kelsey smiled, knowing that today he was centered in a place of tranquility. He was in balance and therefore trusted his ability to answer any unexpected questions quickly without fail.

CHAPTER 2

As Joshua returned from lunch, he checked his messages. He still hadn't heard from his senior team leader, Greg McBride. This was unlike Greg. He knew Greg wasn't fond of him because he felt he had been next in line to run the Production Department before Joshua was hired, but Greg's work ethic would not allow him to let his personal feelings override his duties.

Greg was the one whom everyone in the department respected. He had longevity and experience. His only setback was that he had never finished college. He had been passed over for promotion more than once because of his lack of academic credentials.

Joshua knew that if he could win Greg's respect, the rest of the department would follow suit. As Joshua pondered his situation, there was a knock at the door.

He looked up. "Yes?"

Susan stuck her head through the door.

"Have you had lunch?" Susan asked casually.

"Yes, just got back."

"Too bad."

"What is it?

"I need to talk," Susan responded quietly.

"Come in. Close the door."

Susan entered and sat opposite Joshua's desk. Being the two newest department heads in the company had given them a common ground upon which to build a work relationship that was evolving into a friendship. They were now on a level where they confided in one another with their professional concerns.

It was obvious to Joshua that Susan was struggling with her thoughts.

"What's on your mind?"

"You know, I don't think Ed likes me."

Joshua held eye contact with Susan. He also sensed a lack of support from Edward, but had not revealed it to anyone. He considered the risk of revealing it now to Susan. He had been too trusting in his past positions and had paid the price for revealing his inner feelings. He had vowed not to let this happen again.

"Oh, really?" Joshua asked lightly.

"Really."

"How so?"

"I don't know. I just get this feeling whenever I'm around him. Every time I speak with him, he makes me feel like I'm being a nuisance," she said. "I hope it's just his personality and not something I need to worry about—like sabotage."

Joshua was inclined to agree with Susan's assessment and had similar concerns, but he kept silent.

"So what do you think?" Susan asked, looking worried.

"I don't know," Joshua shrugged.

Susan felt exposed and rejected. She had shared her feelings but Joshua didn't seem willing to assist.

"Well, what about you? How does he treat you?" asked Susan.

Joshua searched for the right answer.

"Well, he does seem distant, but I assumed that was his personality. It's probably going to take him some time to warm up to us."

Just then Edward entered the office.

****

Konrad felt awkward sitting at a table that was clean but clearly worn out over many years of use at Sam's Cafe. He couldn't remember the last time he had been in a local Mom & Pop restaurant. He had forgotten this side of the world existed. Having never married and having had no children. He had dedicated his entire life to his business ventures. Nonetheless, he found it refreshing to see children running throughout the restaurant while parents chased behind.

"So what sparked your interest? Why did you call, Konrad?" Kelsey asked as they sat down to eat.

"Well, to be truthful, I was in the self-help section of Ben's Book World looking for something to help me turn my company around. I stumbled across your book among the bestsellers. The reviews were so good that I bought the book. After reading it, I was hooked. You seemed to have this uncanny ability to verbalize what people were really thinking but were unable to say."

"So what specifically prompted the phone call?"

"The current state of my company. I think a lot of the problems we are experiencing are directly related to some of the issues you addressed in your book. I wanted to find out what other services you provided."

As he took a bite of his burger, Konrad pondered on how to ask Kelsey for help.

"So in what capacity would you be able to help me revamp my organization?"

Kelsey's eyebrows rose with surprise. Konrad noticed his reaction and searched for a follow-up statement.

"I mean, you do offer seminars and personal consultation?"

"Yes," Kelsey rescued him. "We can discuss the opportunities but, first, what's going on with your company?"

Konrad paused. "Where do I begin? For starters, our revenues have been growing, but profits have been shrinking over the past two years. We have been outbid by our competition not to mention they are providing a more superior service."

As Konrad attempted to organize his thoughts, he thought of the defining situation that had precipitated his company's current decline.

"Actually, I know where it all started. We've yet to recover from this incident. We placed a bid on a major contract to provide a major retail chain with its own private label.

"We had included two subcontracting companies as part of the proposal we submitted. Once we were awarded the contract we ran into trouble paying one of the subs because our initial bid was so low. That's actually how we won the contract—we underbid everyone else. I couldn't afford to lose another major contract. The Board of Directors was already recommending a restructuring if things did not turn around. I told the team to win the contract at all cost, but I just didn't understand what 'all costs' meant to some of the company's employees.

"I now realize as the leader of my company, I am responsible for this incident. In any case, to fulfill our obligations, we took our employees from a 40-hour work week to a 45-hour work week. I knew of the potential increase in work hours, but I didn't know about the specific terms regarding the subcontracting companies. I was suddenly faced with jeopardizing our contract or not fulfilling our obligations to one of the subcontractors. Of course, I had to cut one of the subs out. I wasn't happy with the decision, but I couldn't jeopardize my employees' jobs.

"I was really unhappy with myself for letting things get to this point, but I had trusted those surrounding me. I fired our VP of Business Operations manager for withholding the subcontracting terms. That move gave me a little breathing room with the Board of Directors. I later heard the former VP was taking direction from my COO, and that he had assumed that I was aware of everything. My COO of course denied it. He has been with me from the start, and I want to believe him, but I'm just not sure what to believe. Ever since then, morale has dwindled. People are working longer hours and getting paid less. It's been downhill from there."

Konrad continued eating his burger while wondering what was going through Kelsey's mind.

Kelsey was silent. He could feel Konrad's anticipation. He briefly entertained the thought of forcing a statement, but he knew better. No responses were surfacing. Then suddenly a question popped into his head.

"Konrad, are you married?"

****

"Excuse me, did I interrupt anything?" Edward said as he entered Joshua's office.

Susan averted her eyes.

"No, we had just finished lunch and were catching up." Joshua quickly attempted to cover for Susan's awkward silence.

As Susan prepared to leave, Edward stood in the doorway and addressed both Joshua and Susan.

"No, please stay," Edward said. "I wanted to speak with both of you."

Edward sat in the chair beside Susan. Joshua tried to avoid making eye contact with Susan for fear that Edward would guess they had been discussing him unfavorably.

"Let me start by saying that I think you two are doing a wonderful job thus far."

Joshua braced himself. Earlier in his career, he had attended a seminar on managing problem employees. One lesson stuck: Always precede a criticism with a compliment.

"However, I've received some complaints lately from employees in both of your departments," Edward proceeded.

"Is that so?" Joshua replied. "What type of complaints?"

"Generally, the complaints involve how you're interacting with staff. I understand this type of feedback is normal whenever there is a change in management. The bottom line is that while both of you are implementing your new procedures, be sure to stay sensitive to your employees' needs."

Joshua remained silent, but he felt his irritation rise. Edward had questioned Joshua's competency in managing his staff, yet would not provide specific, actionable examples. Joshua could not adequately correct a problem that hadn't been fully identified and for which he and Edward did not have a shared definition.

Edward continued to address both directors. "I have every confidence that you will do well. I know that you two are fairly new to management but don't fret. These are natural transitions."

"Well, how can we improve if we don't know the source of the complaints? This is the first we've heard—and our employees don't feel that they can approach us first?" Susan asked, trying to contain a surge of anger.

Susan had left the statement open, and Edward did not hesitate to close it.

"Oh, don't worry. It's just a situation where they were a little more comfortable with me. That'll change in time and, as far as the complaints, they're really nothing to get worked up about. I'm just here to give you guidance and to prevent potentially bad situations from worsening."

An uncomfortable silence was exchanged between the three.

"Thank you, Edward," Joshua conceded. "I appreciate the heads up. I will definitely keep it in mind as I move forward."

"No problem," Edward replied as he stood up and headed for the door. "Just remember, I'm on your side."

"A wolf in sheep's clothing," Susan muttered after Edward's departure.

"I agree, that didn't feel right," Joshua agreed.

"I've seen his type. He feels threatened. He's still living in the 19th century," Susan said.

"Still, he is the COO. We're going to have to watch our step," Joshua replied, more to himself than to Susan.

"Forget it, Joshua! I've played that game long enough."

"I hear you."

****

"Am I married?" Konrad was taken back and perplexed by Kelsey's question. "No, I'm not. Why do you ask?"

"It's important. Have you ever been married, or were you ever engaged or anything?"

"None of the above." Konrad shook his head.

Kelsey was thoughtful.

Konrad wondered why Kelsey had inquired about his marital status and, surprisingly, he had answered. Had it been anyone else, he would have politely declined to reply. Konrad asked how the personal question related to the business issues at hand.

"Just trying to figure a few things out. Do you work out?"

"Occasionally," Konrad lied. He couldn't remember the last time he had been to the gym.

Konrad noticed Kelsey enter what seemed to be some sort of trance. He assumed Kelsey was daydreaming, but thought it was better not to interrupt him.

The answers were flowing now. Kelsey knew where the change had to begin. He calmly tried to process the information as it entered his mind.

"Konrad?"

The tone of Kelsey's voice had changed slightly requiring Konrad's full attention.

"Do you really want help? Many times people ask for help not realizing what they're really asking for. Oftentimes they can't handle the truth and will sometimes scorn the person who told them. Do you understand what I'm saying?"

Konrad returned Kelsey's stare. He knew the atmosphere had changed. He knew if he said yes, it was quite possible that he could help his company or eventually be forced to resign as CEO. Either way, he knew he was no longer in control, so why not? Everything in him was resisting so he could default back to life as usual, but the force was too strong.

"Yes, I understand."

"So you want to proceed?"

"Yes, I do," Konrad nodded.

"Good," Kelsey sat back in his chair. "My first bit of advice is quite simple. GET A LIFE! You are completely out of balance."

"What?" Konrad exclaimed.

"That's right, Konrad. If you take a look around, nature will teach you all you need to know. You've got summer, spring, winter, fall, night and day, sunshine and rain. Nothing ever stays the same. Life is always evolving. Too much of one thing is never good. With you it's work, work, work, and more work."

I'll be damned. Konrad thought to himself. *I'm coming to him for advice about my company, and he's telling me how incomplete my personal life is? If this is the type of service I can expect, I am glad I found out early. I might as well end this nonsense now.*

Kelsey could see Konrad was struggling with his comment.

"The key is balance. If all we ever got was sunshine, nature would eventually suffer for lack of water. It's the same with you. If all you ever do is focus on work, it will eventually take its toll. You will find yourself constantly being drained, both mentally and physically. Next come smoking, drinking, and other self-destructive habits. When bad habits become a crutch, it's just a matter of time."

"Matter of time for what?" Konrad asked. This exchange was turning stranger by the minute.

Although Kelsey was listening, he had drifted back to a defining moment in his life when he had reached a point of profound understanding of the nature of crisis. He called this understanding the "Evolution of Crisis."

Being taught to comply with the instructions of his parents and others in positions of authority, Kelsey had grown accustomed to terms such as "don't do this, don't do that." He evolved by continuing to conform to both the written and unwritten rules and behaviors exacted by society. Automatically and unquestioningly accepting rules brought Kelsey to a state of complacency, that is, until he ran into the first of many crises. After realizing the expectations society had ingrained in him offered no solution to his crisis, Kelsey entered states of depression, anger, and sadness.

He observed how others too often dealt with their crisis through negative behaviors such as drinking, smoking, emotional outbursts, workaholism. Kelsey knew these were ultimately futile attempts to mediate and realign themselves with society, which often led to a form of disillusionment and discontent. He found most people lived their entire lives maintaining this tedious balance between complacency and frustration with society's expectations and repeating this cycle over and over again until they reached a point where they needed stronger methods to maintain an emotional balance. Though Kelsey felt that feeling balanced was within reach at the level of discontent, he also found that discontent bred a vulnerability to addiction and a range of vices. He believed that those who made the conscious choice to no longer live in crisis could begin to walk the path toward enlightenment. Kelsey also realized that people get confused and dismissive of the word enlightenment. Simply put, enlightenment means seeking knowledge beyond the normal channels to find solutions that would place them back into spiritual, intellectual, and physical balance.

Kelsey found that without proper balance, and a conscious effort to question ingrained behaviors and expectations, one risked a path of darkness that would ultimately cause excessive abuse to the body and psyche.

"Well, consider this." Kelsey began. "All roads—let me repeat—all roads eventually come to an end."

Konrad recalled how lately he found himself tiring more quickly. His tolerance for work-related issues was diminishing fast. He briefly reflected on the early morning glasses of Scotch to which he had grown accustomed. Maybe Kelsey was right.

Kelsey's Journal: Konrad is at a breaking point. His alcohol use has escalated. His company is sliding into chaos. He is flailing, about to go under, but a current of strength and desire to return to success remain. I can see it in his recent hires, his questioning of Edward, his reaching out to me. This is Konrad's tipping point. If he doesn't break through now, the challenges ahead will engulf him. As my parents once told me, "Help from outside is nothing unless matched with help from within" and right now it appears that Konrad is ready for help.

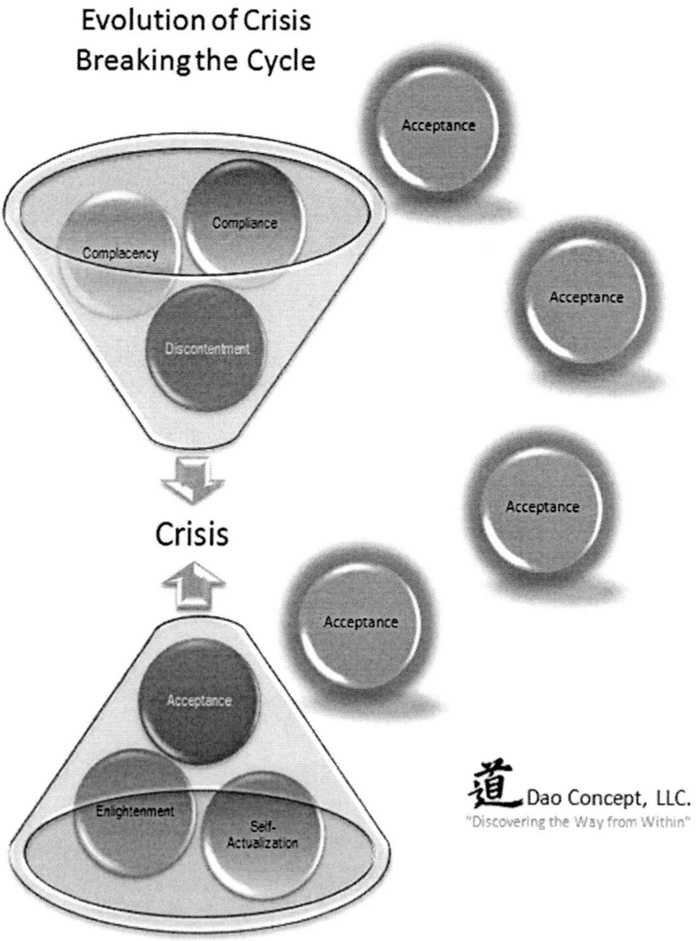

"I cannot give you the formula for success, but I can give you the formula for failure: which is: Try to please everybody"

- Herbert B. Swope

CHAPTER 3

"Greg, good morning," Joshua said as he ended his phone conversation.

"Good morning," Greg nodded, but looking more uptight than usual.

"So is everything ok?"

"Not really. The basement flooded this morning."

"I know that's a nightmare," said Joshua, having had the same experience.

There was an awkward silence as Joshua pondered what to say. He was slightly intimidated by Greg's emotionless expression. In fact, it was his lackluster disposition that inspired Joshua to use a more direct tone.

"Greg," Joshua began, "I've noticed a decline in the quality of your work in the past couple weeks. Is there a problem that I should be aware of?"

"Yes, there is," Greg's facial expression didn't change. "And if you don't mind, I would prefer that you remain unaware of it."

Joshua wasn't ready for that response. As both were African-Americans in a mostly white organization, Joshua had expected an automatic alliance and was irked when it didn't materialize.

"I can accept that for now; however, if your quality of work continues to decline, I will be forced to take some sort of action."

"You're the department manager, right?"

Joshua nodded.

"If something is wrong, my advice is to fix it!" Greg said sharply.

Joshua adjusted himself in his seat. According to how Joshua was raised, Greg's comments were considered a challenge. Joshua's father always taught him that no one should back down from a challenge. A battle could be won or lost through a simple exchange of words. Defending himself was one thing, but in a corporate setting? Greg's near insubordination represented a new situation for Joshua.

"Is that all?" Greg's eyes were piercing.

"Yes," said Joshua, wondering what could be the source of such hostility as Greg left his office.

He was outnumbered in a number of ways, including experience and age. He found himself slightly angered at Greg's boldness and what appeared to be a lack of respect, but deep down inside Joshua felt betrayed.

****

Konrad glanced around Sam's Cafe and noticed there was an entire new set of faces. He hadn't realized they had been there so long.

"I must admit, this meeting has been completely opposite from what I expected," Said Konrad.

Kelsey smiled inwardly. He didn't like being easily categorized with any specific group.

"So what exactly does that mean?" Kelsey asked. "Are you still interested in my services?"

"Of course," Konrad didn't hesitate. "Without a doubt, I would like for you to meet my COO, Edward Starks."

Kelsey nodded.

"When are you free again?" Konrad asked as he pulled out his handheld digitized planner.

"I have no plans for the rest of the day," Kelsey casually answered.

"Oh, really? I mean, great." Konrad sheepishly put his device away. "You'll have to drop me back off at the company anyway. Maybe you can come up and meet Edward then." Kelsey agreed.

Konrad occupied a new state of mind. A sense of peace that had long lain dormant was seeping into his consciousness. He had a slightly sick feeling in his stomach because he feared the new state of mind was temporary. However, he also felt excitement because of the possibility of making sustainable change.

Any other time, Konrad would have been hesitant to allow Kelsey to meet Edward, but today was different. It felt good to be free: free from feeling the need to control situations and their outcomes, letting the chips fall where they may. If Edward liked Kelsey, great. If not, too bad. Konrad liked the freedom he was experiencing. For a brief moment he contemplated the possibility of letting his company fold. Maybe then he could truly begin to live.

****

Susan was fuming. She had already printed a copy of the agenda for this afternoon's staff meeting. She contemplated adding an additional item: Chain of Command. She had specifically communicated to her staff to feel free to approach her with any concerns, but someone had already circumvented her authority and had approached Edward. She was upset, and she wanted to find out who had betrayed her. Suddenly there was a knock at the door.

"Susan?" Konrad stuck his head through the door. "Is this a bad time?"

"No, by all means, please come in,"

"I have someone I'd like you to meet," Konrad smiled.

"OK," Susan answered, curious.

Kelsey entered the office.

"This is Kelsey Knowles, a successful author and executive leadership coach. I am bringing him on board to help us with strategic leadership coaching. Kelsey, this is Susan Lockhart, our Director of Finance."

"Susan, it's my pleasure," Kelsey extended his hand.

"It's nice to meet you." Susan returned his gesture.

"I'm in the exploration phase of defining Kelsey's role, but you will probably be seeing more of Kelsey," Konrad said.

Susan nodded. "I'll look forward to it."

Kelsey sensed Susan's urgency. He knew she was simply just going through the motions, and that she had other more pressing matters on her mind.

"Susan, once again it was a pleasure meeting you," Kelsey said as he retreated toward the door.

"Thank you. You too, Kelsey."

"Susan, let me know if there's anything you need," Konrad said as he followed Kelsey to the door.

Susan relaxed as the door closed behind them. Suddenly her thoughts were clearer. She decided not to add Chain-of-Command to the agenda, as it could be considered an extreme reaction. However, she did not plan on letting her staff completely off the hook either. She would squeeze a comment in somewhere.

Kelsey's Journal: Behind Susan's professional veneer is fear of inadequacy that is not as well-concealed as she believes. She overcompensates and chronically is on edge. Knowledge versus experience has always been a battleground for the blue and white collar workers. Both offer a wealth of tools to effectively do our jobs, but those who learn to integrate both by properly utilizing their resources always obtain a strategic and tactical advantage. Unfortunately for Susan, she has yet to learn this lesson and she utilizes defensiveness when her authority is challenged. She is highly competent, yet like most people she is incomplete, as her personal life is undecorated, unfulfilling. In Susan's transformation, she will replace quiet desperation with confidence in her life as a whole, not just during work hours. My goal with Susan is to help her live a balanced life. Without this change, she will remain a shell.

Edward's door was already open as Konrad and Kelsey approached.

"Edward, how are you?" Konrad asked as he entered the office.

What is Balance?

- ❑ Are you physically healthy?
- ❑ Do you feel healthy?
- ❑ Do you have a mechanism to physically be able to channel stress?

道 Dao Concept, LLC.
"Discovering the Way from Within"

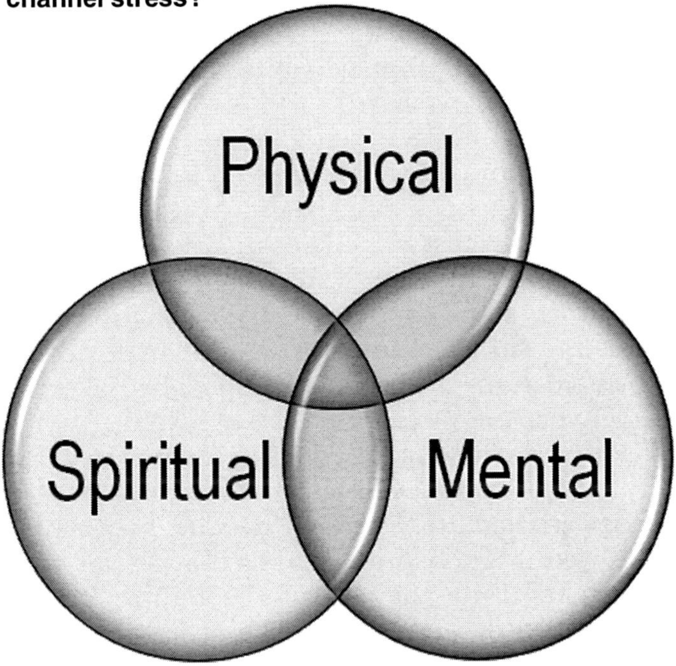

- ❑ How do your interact with your fellow neighbor?
- ❑ How do you interact with the environment?
- ❑ How do you feel about yourself?

- ❑ Result of planning should be clarity of thought
- ❑ How do you react to stress? Are you a Tiger or a Dragon?
- ❑ Types of Mediation
- ❑ Knowing when not to fight is just as important as knowing how to fight

"Time is neutral and does not change things. With courage and initiative, leaders change things."

- Jesse Jackson

"Fine, thanks." Edward barely glanced up from his work. He stood up as he noticed Kelsey.

"This is Kelsey Knowles. Kelsey, this is our Executive Vice President and Chief Operating Officer, Edward Starks."

"Edward, it's my pleasure," Kelsey extended his hand.

"Mr. Knowles, your reputation precedes you," Edward commented as he shook Kelsey's hand.

Kelsey started to ask Edward how he knew him, but he had a feeling that he would have put Edward in an uncomfortable position.

"Thank you," Kelsey nodded.

"Do you mind if we sit down, Edward?" Konrad interceded.

"Not at all. Please, do sit down."

"Edward, our meeting went well, and I plan to work with Kelsey in some capacity in the near future. I think he can be a great asset to us as we realign our company. I have asked him to submit a proposal to assist us in the endeavor."

"Good," Edward replied as he searched for the authenticity to support his words.

Kelsey immediately sensed deceitfulness. In times past, he would ignore the warning signals for the sake of giving people the benefit of the doubt. But things were different now. He always listened to his instincts.

Suddenly Edward stood up.

"Konrad, I just remembered that I have a doctor's appointment in 30 minutes. I've got to leave. You know how that traffic is on Route 66."

"Yes I do," Konrad replied, trying to hide his irritation.

"Kelsey, it was a pleasure to meet you, and I do apologize for the interruption."

"No problem," Kelsey replied calmly.

Kelsey respected Edward for at least squirming out of the meeting rather than sitting and pretending.

Kelsey's Journal: It remains to be seen how much of Edward's motivation is dedicated to preserving the status quo versus his quest for personal power. However, the measure of a man is in his character. An employee who resists change can become an advocate for a new, successful direction if guided by a strong moral compass. Kelsey's instincts warned him that this was not the case here. Most people resist change because they are afraid of the unknown. Very few embrace it. Once confronted with a radically new idea, employees will do one of the following:

1. Resist and only lobby for incremental changes to the status quo. (This tactic usually ensures job security and the individual is spared the pain of growing, but at what cost to the organization and themselves.)

2. Embrace the change because they truly see the benefit for the company, shareholders, and themselves

3. Sit back and say nothing and just follow the crowd until they understand if the initiative will succeed or fail. Typically these employees unconsciously offer passive resistance by not participating at a level that will ensure the project's success

These are the very reasons why so many initiatives, although great in theory, never succeed.

Susan slowly scanned the conference room which was occupied with the members of her department. She had just covered the last item on her agenda and was contemplating how to address the complaints she had received through Edward.

"Any questions?" Susan asked the group.

Silence.

"Well, I have one more issue I would like to discuss. I would like to remind everyone that if you have any problems or issues with anything regarding this department, I have an open door policy. I encourage you to feel free to approach me and address any concerns. Thank you."

She noticed a few people glance awkwardly at one another, but it appeared more innocent than compunctious.

****

Joshua found himself daydreaming during his metro ride home. He barely noticed the high-rises that populated Rosalyn as the train emerged from underground onto the bridge joining DC and Virginia.

He discovered his new-found rivalry with Greg to be very unsettling. He was also irritated for even allowing himself to be consumed with work-related issues after working hours. He had promised himself never to allow the two to mix.

He wondered what he could do to take his mind off work and decided to call his girlfriend, Karla. He found her cheerful greeting comforting.

"What's up, baby," Joshua smiled.

"Nothing much. What's up with you?"

"Missing you," Joshua replies while noticing another female.

"That's sweet."

"So what have you got planned for the evening?" Joshua asked.

"Going to the gym, then home for dinner. That's it. Why, do you need to relieve some stress?"

Karla knew Joshua all too well after having dated him for two years.

"Stress?" Joshua smirked. "What are you talking about? Can't a guy just call his girl to say 'hey'?"

"I'll see you tonight," Karla replied, then hung up.

Joshua smiled with appeasement.

****

Konrad breathed a sigh of relief as he fell back into his recliner. It had been a good day, a productive day. At least it felt like a productive day. He wondered how, since he didn't get any actual paperwork done. Regardless, he felt better this evening than he had in the past few months.

As he scrolled through the cable stations heading toward the CNN, he paused as he noticed a cartoon.

"Fred, from The Flintstones. Wow, it's been a long time," he thought.

He decided to stop there. He laid his head back and fell asleep.

****

Kelsey smiled as he reflected on the day. It was a good day. Everything had gone more or less as expected. His plans didn't always go so smoothly. Regardless of his level of efficiency, he still found failure frustrating. It took him fifteen years in the corporate world to figure out that perfection is evasive. Just when you think you have one process down, a new dynamic introduces itself. Kelsey had covered a lot of ground in his career. He quickly climbed the ladder of success and had managed a $5 billion budget in a Fortune 500 company. However, his career ascent had come at a stiff price, a price that ultimately forced him to make life-changing decisions.

Back then, Kelsey had been at the end of his rope. He was successful at his job. He was competent and efficient based on what the outside world perceived, but internally he was self-destructing. Kelsey had gained over 50 pounds and he was only sleeping on average three to four hours per night. A 16 to 18 hour workday was not unusual. Kelsey's personal life was in shambles too. He was trying to please everyone at a very high cost to himself. Having gone through some of the toughest training the military had to offer as an Airborne Ranger, Kelsey always felt that failure was not an option, even if success meant ultimately giving your life for the mission. Kelsey smiled inwardly as he remembered one of his mentors trying to break him of this habit, but breaking years of military training was going to take a while. Thankfully, Kelsey's mentor was patient and did not abandon Kelsey and his "Do or Die" mentality. He tried to teach Kelsey that he would ultimately fail in business if he did not learn to balance the conflicting priorities of the mission with personal choices of lifestyle.

Kelsey reflected later that his crisis and redemption hadn't had discernible beginning and ending points. His decline and rise had taken place incrementally, and on a continuum. He had lost or gained in imperceptible ways over long periods of time. Daily slippage had led him to the bottom. In profound despair, he realized he had a choice: death, or upward. The pilot light of hope in his heart chose upward. In time, the flicker of a matchstick became a torch.

As Kelsey emerged from his destructive ways, he started pursuing Martial Arts in earnest again. This time he tried Hung Gar, a form of Kung Fu, and later Tai Chi, under the instruction of his Sifu, who had trained in China among elite martial artists. Kelsey knew that he had to shed those extra pounds which reminded him of his past, his failures, and his destructiveness. In order to be balanced and in harmony with emotional and mental aspects, he knew that this was a large part of a universal spirit much larger than himself. Becoming physically fit was part of his transformation, like shedding the cocoon.

Kelsey continued his new path of personal transformation. He quit his job as an executive in a privately-held company to start working for a publicly traded Fortune 500 company. Kelsey knew that he could not change himself fully at his existing job. As much as he wanted to change, the people around him would still view him as the same workaholic who would always figure a way to accomplish the mission. At his new job, Kelsey vowed to create balance for himself at the start.

Working out every morning and practicing Tai Chi on the weekends was just the beginning of Kelsey's makeover. He no longer tried to please everyone. He now focused on doing the right things for himself first. He found that if he was happy, then people around him would generally be pleased with him and his performance. He also no longer avoided conflict. Throughout his life, he had tried to find a compromised position to make everyone happy. He realized this strategy ultimately led to disaster.

Compromising on a good strategy was no different than laws that started out noble, but in the end, turned into watered-down, confusing laws that were difficult to implement and enforce.

Six months into Kelsey's personal change, he realized how much his previous life was in shambles. He was obese by any standard and his heart one beat from a heart attack. The daily stress of work was putting him one step closer to the grave. His mentor kept reminding him: *Work is only a hobby, focus on your family. Family is what really matters.* Kelsey's lifestyle change seemed so long ago. Now, through balance and mental clarity, Kelsey could easily see into the heart of a problem and produce a strategy that would not only solve the problem, but provide for growth years later.

Kelsey smiled again when he remembered something a Human Resources Manager once told him. "Kelsey, most of your peers perceive you as arrogant. You recognize a problem, work through all the plausible solutions and then start implementing the most logical solution that will have the highest level of success before others even identify the problem. You need to take a step backward and help your peers understand what you have already figured out if you ever want sustainable change."

This ability to simplify complex problems was a gift that Kelsey realized everyone did not have. He also realized that this gift was gained through the achievement of inner balance, which led to mental clarity. Kelsey felt this mental clarity gave him the competitive advantage to deal with typical hurdles in corporate America: risk avoidance; politics; paralysis in meetings; misaligned incentives; and lack of executive vision. He now felt it was his duty to help others achieve that which had transformed his life: a sustainable sense of inner balance to gain mental clarity.

Kelsey felt good about today and the internal conflict that he helped Konrad identify. Konrad's struggle was multi-faceted: the struggle between destructive, but comfortable habits and the unsure and difficult path of building a new life. Exceptionally difficult professional decisions Konrad would need to make and weather. And the challenges ahead that were yet to be identified. Kelsey could not force Konrad to change, but he could create the environment by which change is possible. Konrad now was at the edge of the abyss; Kelsey had to be careful to ensure Konrad did not fall into it.

Kelsey thought of a quote from his favorite author, Terry Goodkind:

Reason is a choice. Wishes and whims are not facts, nor are they a means to discovering them. Reason is our only way of grasping reality – it's our basic tool of survival. We are free to evade the effort of thinking and to reject reason, but we are not free to avoid the penalty of the abyss we refuse to see.

Susan sat on the balcony of her condo located on the 12th floor of a luxurious high-rise building in downtown Rosalyn. She was attempting to focus on the book in her hand but was losing the battle to more important subjects. For instance, Joshua Brown.

She glanced at her watch: 8:36 p.m. She wondered what Joshua was doing now. She wasn't sure why she was attracted to him. Was it because her love life was dry? Was it because they were the newest directors at Reality Solutions together? Regardless, she found herself thinking about Joshua more and more.

She searched for an excuse to call him. Maybe she could tell him about her staff meeting. No, he'd see right through her excuse; reporting on meeting results could wait until tomorrow. Susan poured her fourth glass of Merlot, as the effects from the third glass were just starting to take hold.

Susan's confidence elevated as she reflected on her own accomplishments. She was a department head who owned a condo overlooking one of the most expensive communities in her city. Standing on her balcony overlooking the night lights of the city and holding a glass of expensive wine was a combination for a false sense of power. She yielded. She decided to call Joshua while she still felt confident.

Joshua and Karla were arm-in-arm enjoying a movie when his cell phone rang. His heart stopped as he realized he hadn't change the ring tone to silent. Who would be calling him this late?

"Hello."

"Joshua?"

"Yes, who's speaking?"

"I hope I did not catch you at a bad time. This is Susan, from work."

"Susan? How are you? Is everything ok?"

"Oh yes, I just wanted to tell you how my staff meeting went. Are you busy?"

Joshua shifted in discomfort. "Actually, yes. My girlfriend and I are watching a movie."

Susan's heart sank but she recovered fast.

"Oh, no problem. I'm sorry to disturb you. We can talk tomorrow," she said brightly.

"No, it's ok. Do you need to talk?"

Joshua felt guilty as it dawned on him that Susan was attracted to him. He had thought her interest was just his imagination and even if it wasn't, he chose to disregard it. Now that he had realized that it wasn't his imagination, a warm feeling came over him.

"No, really. It's fine. I'll call you tomorrow," Susan said, closing the phone call.

Susan hung up quickly. Suddenly a cloud moved in and shadowed her excitement, putting the flame out of her brief sense of confidence. She settled back into her chair and finished the rest of her wine.

CHAPTER 4

Konrad was leafing through the Washington Post when Edward entered his office the next morning.

"Good morning, Konrad."

"Good morning, Edward," Konrad replied while wondering how Edward would react the day he'd be confronted about entering his office without knocking.

"Mind if I sit down?" Edward said while flopping onto the sofa.

"Go ahead," said Konrad neutrally.

There was an awkward moment of silence as Edward battled with what he was about to say, and Konrad realized there was something on Edward's mind.

"I'll just come out and say it," Edward blurted. "Are you really serious about this guy Kelsey? What good could he possibly do for our company?"

Konrad was infuriated. Not because Edward challenged his leadership, but because Edward arrogantly assumed he knew how to fix all the problems of his company. Konrad stood up to close the door to his office. Edward followed his movements intently.

"First," Konrad began, "why is it that you always challenge my decisions?"

"Challenge your decisions?" Edward retorted. "We've been working together for ten years now. I thought we always made decisions together."

"No, Edward," Konrad calmly stated. "You've always imposed your point of view on me to influence my decisions."

"I don't understand. Where is this coming from?"

Konrad hesitated as he realized that Edward hadn't seen the error of his ways. Konrad blamed himself. He let Edward get away with it for so long that Edward didn't even realize his intrusion was offensive.

"Never mind," Konrad said dismissively. "We can talk about it later. Regarding Kelsey, I haven't completely made up my mind how, but I'm almost sure that I am going to ask him to join our team and assist us with strategic leadership coaching."

"I don't understand," Edward argued. "How is he going to help turn things around? Boost our morale? It's not a morale boost we need. It's dollars!"

"Well, since you seem to have all the answers, Edward, tell me what is it going to take to turn things around?"

Edward backed down realizing that Konrad was upset. He had never seen Konrad react in this manner before. They glanced awkwardly at one another, and then Edward rose to leave.

"I guess now is not a good time to discuss this. Let's go over it later," he said as he left Konrad's office and closed the door behind him.

Konrad reclined in his chair and reflected on recent events. To his surprise he had no regrets for expressing his emotions to Edward. In fact, there was a slight sense of liberation.

****

Susan was sipping on a cup of coffee at her desk when there was a knock at her office door.

"Come in."

"Good morning," Joshua said as he entered.

"Good morning," Susan replied while trying to hide her awkwardness and embarrassment at having called Joshua after hours while he was with his girlfriend.

They exchanged forced pleasantries, and then briefly made eye contact before looking away.

"I am so sorry about last night," Susan began. "I had a lot on my mind and I wanted to talk to someone else who could relate. It's just that Edward got me so frustrated."

"No, everything's cool," Joshua interrupted.

"No, really," Susan continued. "I'm sorry again to have disturbed you. I just had stuff on my mind."

"No, really, Susan," Joshua reassured her. "It's all good."

Their eyes met and locked.

"Call anytime you want," Joshua assured.

Joshua headed toward the door.

"Thanks," Susan said as he left.

Her spirits were lifted. Joshua had just confirmed that he liked her too.

****

Kelsey took the time to study other drivers that surrounded him as he sat in the stop-and-go traffic on Highway 95. He didn't miss the stress, tension, and constant influx of emotions. He smiled to himself as he watched others struggling to find ways to cope. He felt a sense of compassion.

Kelsey's first successful book and the executive leadership coaching business that followed afforded him the luxury of not having to return to the corporate environment, at least not as a regular employee. Konrad had hired Kelsey as a consultant for the next three months. Kelsey's job was to identify flaws and assets in Konrad's management staff as it related to strategy and tactical initiatives, providing solutions to drive profits upward. Most people just did not recognize the extent of the effort behind "providing solutions."

Kelsey's real job was to *help people change so they could create their own solutions for the future*. This was the only way change would be lasting. Most consultant firms are successful based on identifying problems and offering solutions. Consultants often offer temporary solutions, but companies ultimately fail to receive full benefit because most consultant companies fail to address the people and change in leadership necessary to create a lasting change in company culture so that transformation is sustainable. Kelsey thought back to when his publishing and consulting career were simply thoughts in his mind. Some might think it an overused cliché to say that Kelsey wanted to become an executive leadership coach to help people, but that is exactly how he felt. The thought of going out on his own was a commitment Kelsey once feared and avoided, but no longer. After his transformation, he had come to accept that consulting and educating were the reasons for his existence on earth and once he had accepted his fate and path, he had come to peace with himself.

Kelsey had renewed life, renewed energy and a sense of purpose that only comes with knowing the nature of the ultimate mission that one's life is meant to fulfill. It had been a long, sometimes seemingly hopeless road, but his faith had fueled him, even when his circumstances appear to dictate otherwise. He remembered when he used to imagine being an executive leadership coach as he sat in traffic on this very highway, and now it was a reality. In about 15 minutes, he would be addressing yet another management team on leadership values, fulfilling his dream.

****

A cloud of uncertainty hovered over the conference room as the Reality Solutions executive management team waited for Konrad's arrival. This meeting was announced at the last minute, which naturally had piqued everyone's curiosity. It had happened only twice in the history of Reality Solutions. Edward sat in the seat closest to where Konrad would be sitting. His evasive demeanor didn't help to assure anyone.

"Good morning, everyone," Konrad addressed his management team as he took his seat.

Joshua and Susan sat side-by-side as they always did, alongside a host of other directors and upper level management. "For the past five quarters, we have fallen short of our projected profit goals. I have attempted to address the possible reasons for this decline. However,

I have not succeeded. For the second year in a row, we will be unable to distribute bonuses."

Konrad paused and visually circled the meeting table.

"I am forced to seek other alternatives in helping us solve this problem. As of today, I have hired Kelsey Knowles, an Executive Leadership Coach, to assist members of my staff in achieving business focus on the critical areas that will immediately help the bottom line."

Edward shifted in his seat.

"Kelsey's job will be to meet with every department head to assess strengths and weaknesses in individual management styles and propose techniques to help make each of us become more effective managers, starting with me. Kelsey will have three months to effect positive change. I am asking each of you to give him your total cooperation."

Konrad surveyed his staff carefully.

"Are there any questions?"

One of the managers slowly raised his hand and said, "Does this mean it's possible we could lose our jobs?"

Konrad didn't answer right away. He hadn't prepared himself for that question.

"The goal here," he began, "is to reach a state of profitability again. Hopefully that doesn't mean firing anyone. However, I'm willing to do whatever it takes to see improvement."

With no further questions pending, Konrad thanked his staff, and then left the conference room. Everyone sat still, stunned. Slowly, people rose from their chairs and exited the conference room. There was an undertone of restlessness and a mixture of disappointment and uneasiness.

****

As Kelsey entered Reality Solutions, he was warmly greeted by the receptionist. But he could sense uneasiness in the air. In the past, he would have ignored that which wasn't explicitly defined, but being presently in tune with his surroundings, Kelsey's instinct served as a warning. Konrad's staff knew he was coming. They were bracing themselves because they rightfully feared for their jobs. Change was afoot, and change always brings confrontations. Smiling inwardly, Kelsey remembered something his first manager out of the military taught him. "Change is coming. Catch the wave or drown."

****

"Did you see Edward?" Susan commented as she sat across from Joshua's desk.

"Did I? He didn't seem happy at all," Joshua said.

"No. Something's up. Something is going on," Susan speculated. "I think Konrad and Edward are at odds."

"I doubt it," Joshua replied. "They've been working together for years."

"I know, but you never noticed how Edward constantly overshadows Konrad's decisions?" Susan asked.

Joshua disagreed. "It isn't like that. They have an understanding. Like I said, they've been working together for years."

Susan was slightly disgusted.

"You know what your problem is, Joshua? You can't see the obvious."

Joshua was unsure if Susan was referring to Konrad and Edward or Susan and him.

"I guess you're right."

Joshua's phone rang. It was Konrad, requesting that Joshua immediately proceed to a nearby conference room. Joshua replied in the affirmative, feeling slightly alarmed.

****

As Joshua entered the room, Kelsey stood up to greet him.

"I'm Kelsey Knowles," Kelsey extended his hand.

"Joshua Brown," Joshua returned the handshake.

"Pleasure to meet you," Kelsey nodded.

"Likewise."

Kelsey felt somewhat awkward as he took his seat. First meetings were always like this, sitting across from an individual whom he knew was intimidated by him. He relaxed and allowed the tension to build just a bit longer before engaging.

"First of all," Kelsey began, "I'm not feeling this environment. It's a bit stuffy in here. Do you want to grab a cup of coffee?"

Joshua sat back in curiosity. He had expected Kelsey to open a folder and ask a lot of questions from a pre-prepared list.

"Sure," Joshua agreed.

****

"So how do you like the corporate life at Reality Solutions?" Kelsey took a sip from his cup.

Joshua was hesitant to respond. He didn't want to say anything that could possibly incriminate him. Kelsey sensed his uneasiness.

"Honestly, I don't know yet. It's too early to tell. But I can tell there are politics involved."

Kelsey nodded.

"So where are you from?" Kelsey asked.

"Alexandria. I grew up in the valley. Are you familiar with that area?"

"No, don't think so."

"Well, it's a lot better now; but when I was growing up, the neighborhood was heavily drug-infested. I'm actually the first in my family to graduate from college. I'm one of the lucky ones."

"I see. So where did you go to school?"

"Howard University."

"Very nice."

Kelsey felt good. He was making progress. He knew that before helping someone, it was a good idea to get to know that person first. Kelsey recalled a comment from a long-time mentor and friend: "If you can help a person deal with the personal issues, most of the time the business issues go away."

Edward sat in his office leafing through papers. He didn't see the text on the papers because he was blinded by resentment. He felt betrayed by Konrad. Konrad had always confirmed his approval before making a major decision. Bringing Kelsey onboard was not in the plan. Now he was worried. Where did he stand? Was his job in jeopardy?

****

"So tell me about your project, Kelsey," Joshua inquired. "What is your role?"

"Suffice it to say, my goal is to teach the value of focus through mental clarity. Depending on a person's individual needs, I employ different techniques to help individuals achieve this clarity. I will teach you how to focus on the 'big problems' and ignore the 'little problems' that seem to take up most of your day."

"So this isn't about downsizing?"

"In order for any company to survive in the corporate world, it has to make money. If that doesn't happen, then yes, downsizing is necessary. My purpose is to help equip the management staff with the tools to ensure success."

"So this isn't about cutting back and saving money at all?" asked Joshua, slightly surprised and relieved.

"Don't get me wrong, Joshua. I am not going to make those types of recommendations, but you might. As I stated, I am here to help you focus on providing a clear strategic direction so your entire staff learns the value of focus." Kelsey watched Joshua carefully.

Now that Joshua's primary fears had been assuaged, Kelsey decided to be more direct with his questions. Previously, Joshua's fears might have prevented him from answering truthfully.

"So Joshua, what do you do for Reality Solutions?"

"I'm the Director heading the Production Department. We're responsible for processing and managing all the orders that come in. We also follow up with any complaints that are filed," Joshua said.

"So basically your department is the nerve center of the company," said Kelsey.

"Basically," nodded Joshua, glad that Kelsey quickly assessed the importance of his department.

"How is the morale?"

Joshua paused, searching for the best answer.

"Pretty low right now."

"What would you say is the cause?" Kelsey queried.

"It's hard to say. I'm fairly new, and before I arrived the morale was already declining. I basically walked into a big mess."

"How does your staff view you? Do you have their respect?"

"I think so for the most part but, honestly, I think their mentality is 'Do what I have to do and drive on.' There is this one employee, however, Greg McBride. He doesn't like me. He was passed over for my position because he doesn't have a college degree. He's bitter, and he's taking it out on me."

"So what are your thoughts?" Kelsey asked while ensuring they maintained eye contact.

"About what exactly?" *What do I really think? Nothing positive!* Joshua thought to himself.

"Greg taking it out on you."

Joshua shrugged. "He has to deal with it."

Joshua paused to notice Kelsey's reactions.

"So how would you handle it?" Joshua inquired.

"Do you really want to know?"

"Yes, please be candid." Joshua was curious as to what Kelsey would say.

"Make him your right hand man."

"Excuse me?" Joshua wasn't sure he had heard correctly.

"That's right," Kelsey answered coolly.

"Apparently, Greg is the most experienced employee you have, which means he has a longstanding history there. He holds vital information you need to be equipped with in order to manage that division effectively. Divert Greg's resentment by creating a new title for him. Give him a raise. If you block him out, he could keep vital information from you that could paralyze your progress. He could also spoil your reputation amongst the rest of the employees."

Joshua was stunned and shook his head. "I never looked at it that way."

Kelsey was pleased. He was focused. The answers flowed effortlessly. That's usually how it was when you had clarity. Life was not meant to be hard. We only make it hard because everyone around us keeps telling us how hard life is.

"So, essentially you're telling me to give in and bow down to Greg," said Joshua. "How is that going to look to everyone?"

"No," Kelsey disagreed. "It has nothing to do with losing face or power struggles. You must focus on the big picture. If the company keeps losing money, Konrad will have to consider downsizing. If that happens, everyone loses out. How significant would your and Greg's feud be then? It's true that leveraging your higher position, you could easily defeat Greg by making his life miserable, but is there any honor in that when you're sitting at home jobless? Knowing how to fight is great, but the most important thing about fighting is knowing when not to fight. Why expend your energy on little skirmishes? Once again, learn to focus on the big picture and the little battles become meaningless."

Joshua nodded slowly.

"Where did you learn this approach? They just don't teach this anywhere. Usually we watch the actions of others and emulate what we think is successful, and very few really teach us how to successfully navigate the ranks of Corporate America."

"Experience and a bit of unconventional methods. Let's head back to the office," Kelsey said as he finished his cup of coffee.

Kelsey's Journal: The future of Reality Solutions rests on employees such as Joshua. He embodies the rare blend of practicality and sensitivity. He has had to fight for every inch of his education and career, with few predecessors lighting the way. Yet he does not possess an air of bitterness. The irony is that his greatest challenge lies within where he would expect to find his strongest support. Teaching Joshua that in order to truly gain control of a project, you must first give it away, will be one of the hardest lessons he will face. Although this concept sounds counterintuitive, to master it will help employees not only support the initiative, but truly embrace it.

CHAPTER 5

Back home, Konrad sat back in his recliner and reflected on the days' events. He finally felt as though he was making progress. Though it was true that it could be a while before he saw a profit uptick in his company, he was satisfied that he had made the right decision to strengthen shareholder value. Konrad remembered before the Internet stock market boom when the performance of a company was dictated by the consumer. A company's performance was measured by how much product was sold. In those days, companies created a valuable product that consumers wanted, and consumers with their power of purchase determined who the winner was. Nowadays, Wall Street Analysts were the Shareholders. It was all about the number games and stock prices with the consumer playing an increasingly minor factor in the creation of a strategic vision for the company.

Konrad returned from his reverie to the present. Perhaps it was more the fact that he was beginning to see the value of making decisions based on the good of the ultimate shareholder rather than only pleasing Wall Street with quarter-end results. It felt good not to allow the pressure of external influences to dictate his decisions.

He tried to pinpoint what it was about Kelsey that had influenced him in such a manner. Kelsey had a way of expressing his views without intimidating or making one feel less of a person. In fact, there was something about Kelsey that caused one to aspire to his level of freedom. As Konrad began to doze, he hoped that he could find a way to keep this newfound freedom.

****

"What are you reading?" Karla glanced in Joshua's direction as she exited the shower.

"It's a book called *Decisive Leadership* written by Kelsey Knowles."

"I like that title," Karla said, intrigued.

"The man knows his stuff," Joshua answered.

"Have you met him?"

"I had a cup of coffee with him today. Our CEO hired him as a consultant to teach our staff the value of focus to improve shareholder value."

"Impressive."

"At first I was intimidated because I thought he was hired to help downsize. It happens so much in the corporate world. CEOs hire someone to tell them who to fire. Go figure! But after we talked for a bit, I was really impressed. Kelsey's insights were thought-provoking and really caused me to think beyond my comfort zone. It was almost as if I hadn't had an independent thought in ages." Enthusiasm was evident in Joshua's voice.

Karla climbed into bed beside Joshua and cuddled. "He really made a good impression on you, I guess."

Joshua was thoughtful as he returned her embrace. "Yes, he did."

****

Edward's wife, Julie, could tell her husband was irritated. He hadn't had much to say all evening. He had been more stressed lately. She approached him from behind as he sat in his office chair reading a magazine.

"So what's on your mind, dear?" Julie asked while rubbing his shoulders.

"Not such a good day at work today. I'm sorry. I know I've been distant," Edward answered absently.

"Anything you care to talk about?"

"I don't know. I'm not sure if it'll do any good anyway. The decision has already been made."

"What decision?"

"Konrad just hired this consultant to advise us on so called 'How to achieve better performance results through focus clarity.' Give me a break! Konrad is full of it. If you ask me, I think he should step down and let someone else take the helm. Hiring this guy is just the latest in a series of serious mistakes he has made. A consultant 20 years my junior is to determine the fate of Reality Solutions?"

"Edward, please. You shouldn't let these things upset you like this," Julie consoled.

"I know, I know, honey."

****

Susan was in good spirits as she prepared for work. She didn't attempt to overanalyze her contentment but, instead, decided to maximize the moment. She settled on wearing the new designer business suit she had bought a month ago. She was feeling confident.

Susan's spirits continued to lift during her drive to work. She noticed the little boys playing tackle football while waiting for their school bus. She couldn't help but wonder how many times she had previously passed them without noticing them.

As she entered her office she noticed the red message light blinking on her office phone.

"Could you set aside some time to meet with Kelsey this morning?" asked Konrad's voice from the speaker phone. "I would like for you to meet with him at 10 a.m. this morning."

Susan sighed. She wasn't looking forward to this meeting. She had her day already planned out. Plus, she was backed up with emails. Her heart sank as a portion of her good spirits flew away. She just wasn't in the mood to be involved in a conversation of that type.

****

Kelsey sat in the conference room, fumbling through notes while awaiting Susan's arrival. He was reserved.

He never knew what type of reaction to expect from initial meetings.

"Good morning," Susan greeted Kelsey as she entered the room.

"Good morning," Kelsey replied while standing up and extending his hand. "I'm Kelsey Knowles."

"Susan Lockhart."

"I believe we met the other day."

"Yes. We did," Susan answered as she shook his hand.

"It's a pleasure to see you," Kelsey began. "I have heard some good things about you."

"Thank you." Susan was flattered while attempting to remain professional.

"Please sit down and make yourself comfortable."

Susan nodded while taking a seat across the table from Kelsey.

"First of all, let me begin by saying this is not an interview to determine whether or not your current position is needed. I'm not sure how Konrad explained it, but I seem to be getting that type of reaction from individuals."

"I can imagine," Susan agreed. "Konrad was reserved in regards to your purpose here and people tend to suspect the worst. Layoffs are also an underlying fear, given the difficulties Reality Solutions has faced in the past couple of years." Susan was toeing the company line, giving nothing away.

Kelsey considered Susan. He acknowledged Susan's physical attractiveness. Susan was intelligent, but she was hiding behind her professional persona.

Kelsey knew he would have to be patient with her. He could tell that if he rushed in offering suggestions she would become defensive. She would be looking for formulas and strategies presented externally to further her career. That's the way she had been programmed to think, probably by her parents, society, college and possibly other business associates. Kelsey knew he'd have to try another approach that could not be interpreted as an intrusion.

"Susan, I'd like to ask you a question, and I hope you don't mind my bluntness. I'm really not one for idle conversation in moments like this."

Susan leaned slightly forward as she nodded.

Kelsey knew he had her attention. He knew she appreciated his bluntness, because that was her style as well.

"Of all of your years of education, what event, person, knowledge, or experience stands out as the most influential as it pertains to your life today?"

Susan sat back in her seat. She was baffled but impressed. *An unexpected question, indeed.* Yet, it pleased her because it presented a challenge. *What was his motive for asking this type of question? But better yet, what is the answer?*

Kelsey maintained eye contact as Susan pondered. He knew eye contact was important at this point. He knew that as her eyes circled the room searching for an answer that they would occasionally land back on Kelsey's to make sure this is really what he wanted to know.

Suddenly Susan's eyes stopped wandering. She had discovered the answer. Now she was wondering whether to reveal it, or mask the truth.

"This is not a test, Susan," Kelsey sensed her hesitation. "You're not being graded. This is just two normal people talking face to face."

"It was a class I took while pursuing my MBA. I had written a paper where my job was to present to a company new procedures in streamlining their Accounts Payable process. I had so much fun while writing that paper. I was able to interview managers from various companies, and I also discovered that I believe current management processes are traditional and outdated and need to be revamped and integrated with today's technology. In fact, I question the need of multiple levels of management in a time where today's technology allows us to conveniently manage ourselves."

Susan felt a new level of freedom after saying that. In fact, she suddenly felt a new sense of focus and purpose. She remembered the passion and energy she felt when she first started with Reality Solutions. She was suddenly anxious to end the meeting and return to work to take advantage of this newfound energy.

"That's actually all I have for now, Susan," Kelsey said sensing her anxiousness to end the meeting. Kelsey actually wanted to understand what it was that Susan had learned, but decided not to push it. He would have his answer in time. "I'll be in touch for our next meeting. Have a great day," Joshua concluded.

As Susan stood to shake his hand, she realized she was slightly puzzled and unsure of what had just transpired. In a matter of minutes, Kelsey had motivated her by barely saying a word. She came into the meeting thinking she was in for the typical consultant brain drain: "What do you do?" "How long does it take?" "Is there a more efficient way to do things?" But instead, Susan departed actually looking forward to the next meeting. *Not bad.* She thought. Kelsey might just be all right.

Kelsey's Journal: Susan may actually embrace transformation quicker than the others. She is already seeking; an incomplete life is easier to change than a life ingrained in predictable mediocrity. Some people have to experience profound pain before they are willing to make a change.

Susan sat on her balcony sipping a glass of wine, once again alone. Many thoughts rushed through her mind, but one loomed larger than the rest. *Who was Kelsey Knowles?* He was accomplished many years beyond his age. He was smart. He was good-looking and charismatic. He was confident, intelligent, and fearless. She knew he was well-educated, but his perceptiveness seemed rooted in something deeper, something she didn't have access to, but she wanted. *I want to be able to walk into a room and command respect without being perceived as a bitch because I demand excellence. I have met Kelsey twice and both times, although each meeting was brief, he truly sensed and assessed the environment and acted accordingly. Now that's a skill that I want and I will not stop until I master it.*

Susan reflected on her past. She had grown up in a low income family in a mostly middle to upper middle class community. Her father worked as a plumber, and her mother worked in a day-care center. Although both of her parents did well in school, her father had to drop out of high school in his senior year to help his family. Her mother never had an opportunity to attend college because she lacked the means to pay for it. Because of her parents' lack of formal education, neither could find a suitable position in the corporate world.

Susan had always secretly been ashamed of her working class roots. Many of her friends' parents were engineers, lawyers and directors in the corporate world. Susan often found herself avoiding conversations where she had to reveal her parents' professions, which had driven her to excel in school. The prospect of inheriting her parents' limited opportunities heightened the importance of education in her mind and motivated her to work through any job she could find every summer to pay for her education. Her sheer determination drove her accomplishments and achievements. Susan held an undergraduate degree from Columbia University and a MBA from Duke, and was now a Director at a fairly young age. Susan felt she had to work twice as hard as her male peers because of her gender. She felt her physical attractiveness at times undermined her efforts. After years of hard work to ascend to her current position, Susan felt something was still missing.

Now she sat on her balcony, conflicted. She had accomplished her goals, but true happiness eluded her. She felt empty. Then she met Kelsey. She remembered something he had said in their brief meeting, that happiness sometimes lives outside of corporate achievement. *How dare he intrude into her life boasting of a happiness unrelated to climbing the* corporate ladder *which was the foundation of her life? What everyone lives and kills for: to be successful!* Susan suddenly harbored a slight resentment toward Kelsey; but it was too late. Her curiosity had been aroused. She would have to find out more.

****

Kelsey drove down the George Washington Parkway traveling at 60 mph. The driver's side window was down about halfway. Kelsey welcomed the light rain as the tiny refreshing droplets hit his face. To his left, he noticed the trees swaying from the wind. The sky was slightly overcast. Kelsey loved these types of days. They reminded him of the trips he use to take with his auntie when he was a boy, sitting in the back seat with the window slightly down, allowing the rain to pelt against his face.

Kelsey knew that he was on the right path. It wasn't just about reaching the destination. It was about enjoying the journey.

****

"Anything I should be concerned about regarding this past week's assessments?" Konrad asked.

Edward sat across from him leafing through his reports.

"Same as last week," he replied. "I'm still getting complaints from Susan and Joshua's departments."

"What kind of complaints?"

"Minor issues. Changes in procedures."

"Are these complaints related to employees adjusting to new management styles, or is it something that I should really be concerned about?" Konrad asked.

"At this point, I'm really not sure. I've spoken with both directors off-line, and I think they have a clear understanding of what is needed. I can investigate further if you wish," Edward answered.

Konrad nodded.

"So what type feedback are you getting regarding Kelsey's interviews?"

Edward took his time to fish for the right words. He wanted to allow this opportunity to tell Konrad that in no way can Kelsey help their employees or their company and that Konrad is wasting his time with Kelsey. On the other hand, he wanted to show his disapproval without offending Konrad.

"Not good," Edward responded grimly.

"Really?" Konrad's eyebrows rose. "How so?"

"Well, I've received a range of comments, none of which are positive. Some think his approach is unorthodox, too personal, less professional."

"Interesting," Konrad pondered.

Edward wondered if the smirk on his face was too obvious. He reveled in being able to give a negative report on Kelsey.

"Well," Konrad began, "I guess that is to be expected. It's our nature to resist change. I've been resisting it for years now. I felt the same way when I first met Kelsey. He was not what I expected, but everything I needed. He pushed me out of my comfort zone and made me answer some tough questions, both professionally and personally. It's still sinking in. Ultimately, I feel my change in perspective will help—even save—this company. But more importantly, I feel that Kelsey is helping me become a more effective leader."

Edward sighed, disappointed, then looked up upon hearing a knock at the door. His disappointment increased when he realized the visitor was Kelsey.

"Good morning," Kelsey said as he entered Konrad's office.

"Good morning," Edward mumbled.

"Good morning, Kelsey," Konrad stood. "We were just talking about you."

"Good news, I hope," Kelsey said extending his hand to Edward.

Edward nodded as he returned his handshake.

"Kelsey, please have a seat."

Kelsey noticed the awkwardness between Konrad and Edward. He made a mental note to pay close attention to this dynamic and how it would affect the overall disposition of the company.

"That's all I had," Edward stood to leave. "I'll leave you two alone," and left the office.

"So how was your commute?" Konrad asked.

"Wonderful," Kelsey replied.

"I wanted to discuss your progress so far." Konrad began. "What is your assessment?"

"Well," Kelsey paused. "It's too early to tell. Right now I am simply getting a feel for your management team. I think people are a little uncomfortable and are not really sure how to receive me. I need to work through that in order to get down to the core issues."

"I see," Konrad nodded. "How long do you think this might take?"

"Not sure. It depends on the individual, but I think that in another few weeks I'll have a more accurate assessment."

"Sounds good," Konrad agreed. "Keep doing what you're doing and let me know how I can help. I have a lot of faith in you."

Kelsey confirmed his commitment and promised to keep Konrad posted.

Kelsey's Journal: Konrad is growing stronger, his step and demeanor more sure. Edward's influence is losing its grip. Konrad is turning the corner. He has chosen to raise the bar and is gaining momentum even quicker than I had hoped. The question is will Edward be able to adjust to the change in culture, let alone lead it day-to-day? My first manager out of the military once led a change campaign and his favor quote was "Catch the Wave or Drown." I feel Konrad now is waiting to see who will rise to the top. This part is easy. Helping Konrad manage through restructuring his organization will be the hard part. The management team at Reality Solutions is a close-knit family. Releasing friends is never an easy task. For Konrad to truly save his company and change the culture this may be a necessary step. Only time will tell.

CHAPTER 6

Susan was preparing for a daily staff meeting when Edward knocked at her door, and asked if she had a few minutes to talk.

"I'm preparing for a staff meeting that starts in ten minutes," Susan advised.

"This won't take long," Edward took a seat. "I'm still getting complaints from your employees."

Susan's complexion turned red as she released a sigh of anger.

"What is it this time?"

"Apparently they don't like some of your new changes in procedures."

"Could you kindly tell me who is complaining? Is it just one person, or more?"

"Your staff came to me in confidence. I'm not at liberty to release that information."

"You're not at liberty to release that information?" Susan asked, failing to conceal her irritation. "What is this, Edward?"

"Look, Susan," Edward began. "Don't get upset with me. I'm not the one complaining."

"Well, who else is there to get upset with? I'm completely in the dark here."

Edward looked away.

"If they're complaining about the procedures, what specifically do I need to address? I thought I was hired by Reality Solutions to make necessary changes to ensure we met Sarbanes-Oxley requirements. You should be worried if the staff doesn't complain. I have a unique management style that differs from the status quo, which I thought you valued when I was hired.

Shouldn't it be everyone's goal to make improvements in the department? We can't do this by staying the course."

"I understand, Susan, but you must remain sensitive to your employees. Some are a lot older and have been used to doing things a certain way for years."

Susan glared at Edward, then looked away.

"Ok, Edward. I'll take a closer look at things."

"Thank you, Susan," Edward replied.

Susan glared at the door after he left. Since her early years in high school, she knew she didn't like being challenged. She was voted as the class vice president during her junior year. The president asked her to show proof how money was spent for the prom dance. Susan was incensed, not because money had been misappropriated— she had saved all receipts— but because someone had the audacity to challenge her morals. She took it personally. No one had ever pointed out Susan's inability to accept input or coaching as a flaw, so her defensiveness became an integral part of her personality. In one sense, it was positive because it drove her to become very detailed in her dealings to prevent others from ever needing to challenge her, but it was also precisely what made a challenge that much more unfounded in her mind.

Susan already knew that half of her employees were older than her. She had taken this into consideration when she began implementing her new procedures. She resolved that whoever was complaining was being completely unreasonable. She knew that the changes she had implemented would improve the department. *So what was the problem? Who was complaining?*

****

Joshua idled at his laptop, mindlessly scanning emails as he waited for Greg to arrive. Joshua had spent a lot of time thinking about his conversation with Kelsey. He had decided to offer Greg the position of an Assistant Director on a probationary period, after which he would receive a salary adjustment once the probationary period was over.

"Please sit down, Greg," Joshua said as he entered. "I wanted to speak to you about something."

Greg complied.

"Greg, let me begin by saying, I have nothing personally against you. I don't know why you are upset with me and, at this point, unless you let me in on your secret, I can't afford to care."

Greg's faced immediately displayed his obvious offense to Joshua's statement.

"Please hear me out," Joshua requested. "Reality Solutions posted this job, not me. It's easy to sit there and take it out on me, but did I personally do anything to you?"

When Greg did not answer, Joshua continued.

"My mentor once taught me that when we are upset at someone, if we take the time to look at that emotion, we will realize that we are only projecting our own feelings toward the other person. So in your case, I can only assume that you are angry at me for being hired to run this department, even though you have the experience, technical expertise, and the respect of the team. So why did they not promote you?"

Several minutes of awkward silence passed, but Joshua did nothing to alleviate Greg's discomfort. Joshua remembered Kelsey had said to be very adamant when confronting Greg. "In order to truly win Greg over, Greg will have to face up to his own demons. If you give Greg the answers, he will not accept any proposed solution because he will still truly feel he deserves your job."

Joshua waited. Finally, Greg angrily looked up and said "What do you want to hear? That I do not have a college degree? There, I have said it! I don't have a degree, but I know I am far more qualified to run this department than you. I am so tired of getting passed over because I do not fit in that perfect cookie cutter world like you and my last two bosses."

"So are you going to just sit there and complain and eventually get fired?" Joshua challenged. "Because, let me tell you, this company has much bigger problems than what is going on between us. Or for a change, do you want to do something about it?"

Greg just sat there and thought, *In my entire career, no one has ever spoken to me this bluntly. Should I sit here and take this or just quit?* Greg continued to stare at Joshua. Still shocked, Greg thought, *Something is going on and, at this point, what do I have to lose? At worst, I will at least get a severance package out of this.*

Seeing that he had got Greg's attention, Joshua continued, "Are you interested in being promoted?"

Greg, who was previously looking down, raised his head and met Joshua's stare. "Promoted?" Greg repeated.

"Yes."

"Of course." Greg replied with obvious shock.

Joshua continued. "I have really been struggling with what we should do next here in our department. I can't improve our results here without you. I went to the senior vice president of HR and asked what my options were. Considering your time and performance here at the company, I was able to get you approved for an Assistant Director's position. You already have the respect of all the employees on the floor, so if I announce that they have to report to you, that wouldn't cause any problems."

"OK, Why this sudden mention of a promotion? What's the catch?" Greg asked cautiously.

"I'll admit, Greg," Joshua leaned forward, "no one understands the intricate details of this department better than you, not even me. So we're going to have to work together to turn things around. If we don't, I assure you, we'll all be in the unemployment line, college degree or no degree. Do you understand what I'm saying? Failure is not an option for either one of us."

Greg sat back in his chair.

"So what is your plan?"

"I can give you the title," Joshua began. "But I can't give you the raise. There is simply no money left in this year's budget. But if I can convince you to work extremely hard and efficiently for the next quarter, and if you can convince our department to do the same, then by Christmas, I promise you, we'll all have something to smile about."

Greg pondered Joshua's statement for a moment.

"So you want to give me a title with no money," Greg began. "Then you want me to work twice as hard. And on top of that, convince my co-workers to work twice as hard for the same salary."

"Not harder, but smarter. The department is currently effective, but we are not efficient. To answer your question, yes," Joshua nodded cautiously.

"And if this works, the company will take care of me and ensure a raise?"

"Look, Greg. If this works, we will all come out looking good. That opens doors for me in this company as well. I learned from one of my previous managers to never leave a job without having a strong candidate to backfill your spot. Who do you think my recommendation would be? There is one concern however, that we need to address," Joshua said.

****

Susan's body language made it clear to her employees that she was upset. She sat in her chair and took a deep breath.

"An issue has come to my attention," she began. "I've been advised that several of our team members have gone above my head to complain about procedural changes in this department. I'd like to review chain-of-command. That means if you have a problem, you come to me first."

She addressed her staff as she looked around at everyone who was sitting at the table. "If we can't resolve it, then we go to the next level of management. Now I thought I had made it clear that I have an open door policy, but someone chose to go over my head. I would appreciate it if from this point on, you would direct your complaints to me. Are there any questions?" Everyone sat silently. As Susan began addressing the subsequent meeting topics, she wondered why getting feedback from this group seemed harder than pulling teeth.

****

Kelsey sat in his bedroom staring out the window into the starlit sky as he stretched and prepared for his Tai Chi workout. It was 5:30 a.m. It felt good to make time for himself. Five years ago he would have already been at work preparing for the day's events before everyone else arrived. If he wasn't trying to meet a deadline, he'd be preparing for the next. Relaxation was not even a thought. He had to stay ahead of the competition at any cost.

Kelsey glanced at the spot where the picture of his ex-fiancé, Stephanie, once stood. Kelsey had once been lost, both personally and professionally. To everyone else, it seemed he was on top of his game with an attractive fiancé and a prominent position as a vice president with a top Fortune 500 company. His peers assumed he would eventually be the youngest Senior VP in the history of the company. Yet Kelsey felt perpetually disconnected with his surroundings.

"If she could see me now," he thought.

As he was walking to a park nearby, he reflected what started it all and enabled him to be where he was today. It wasn't until Kelsey was introduced to Tai Chi that he was able to get over Stephanie. As tumultuous and stressful as their relationship had been, he had loved her and truly believed they would spend their lives together.

As Kelsey began to understand Chi and how energy flowed throughout the body, he understood why he was so mentally drained. He never got a break: a hard day at work, and then dealing with Stephanie when he finally came home. She only expected perfection from him, a standard of perfection set by her. He was using his energy to accommodate everyone around him, including Stephanie, with nothing for himself. Nor did he know how to replenish the energy. Suffice it to say, Kelsey was slowly dying. His Sifu had showed him how to replenish his energy and always conserve some energy for himself utilizing principles of Tai Chi. So many times in the past, Kelsey had fallen sick because he focused all of his energy into helping others to his own detriment.

Halfway into his workout, the phone rang. Kelsey frowned with irritation as he realized that he'd left the ringer on. He attempted to ignore the ring, but eventually gave in with reluctance.

"Hello."

"Kelsey?"

He recognized that voice. It didn't take long to figure out who it was.

"Stephanie?"

"Of course it's me."

"What a surprise. How have you been?"

"I've been good, and what about you? I know it's a bit early to call but if you are still who I remembered, I figured you were already up and I wanted to make sure that I got hold of you. I just got your number last night and I could not wait any more," Stephanie replied coyly.

"Good," Kelsey replied. "Thank you for asking."

Kelsey was overcome with excitement. He was thrilled to hear her voice.

"So, how did you find me? How did you get this number?"

"Well, that's a silly question to ask, Kelsey. You are a famous writer now, and let's not forget we still have some of the same friends."

"Understood."

"Congratulations on your book."

"Thanks. I appreciate that."

Kelsey was at a loss for words. He was just happy to be hearing her voice again.

"So you did it, didn't you?" Stephanie exclaimed with exaggerated enthusiasm.

"Did what?"

"The book. You said you were going to write it, and you did it."

"Yes, well, I guess I've been fortunate."

There was an awkward silence as Kelsey's euphoria began to wane. He sensed there was more to Stephanie's call than just congratulations.

"So how have you been, Stephanie?"

"Honestly?"

"Yes."

"Missing you."

Silence. Kelsey knew what was next. He knew this moment would come. He had rehearsed his speech, but now that he had the opportunity to recite it, he couldn't bring himself to speak.

"Have you missed me?" Stephanie purred.

"Oh you have no idea."

"Let's do dinner soon, my treat."

Kelsey didn't answer right away. He was on the verge of conceding, but he had already been down this road and knew the outcome. Allowing Stephanie to leave was just as vital to maintaining Kelsey's inner harmony as doing Tai Chi. Stephanie was a leech on Kelsey's psyche. She only wanted what was in her best interest. Now that Kelsey was back in control, he knew what it meant to allow her back into his life. He had come too far to allow anyone to stop him now, including Stephanie.

"I'll be in town for a few days. How about a nice dinner with me at 7:00 p.m. tomorrow night?" Stephanie chirped cheerfully on the other side of the receiver.

"Well, Stephanie, let me ask you something," Kelsey began. "Why haven't you called before now?" he asked, feeling miserable at the mere thought of the past.

"Well," Stephanie stammered, "I knew you were upset with me, and I thought that I was the last person you wanted to hear from."

"Actually, Stephanie, your voice was the only thing I wanted to hear. I wanted to hear you say you were coming back home. You have no idea how many nights I fell asleep staring at the phone, hoping it would ring."

"Kelsey, I had no idea."

"And now you pop back up out of the blue as if nothing ever happened."

Kelsey could feel his emotions getting the best of him.

"Kelsey, it was a tough time for me too. You had promised me so many things, and then suddenly you were leaving your job? What was I suppose to do?"

Silence.

"How about believe in me?" Kelsey said.

Silence.

"You know what, Stephanie? I don't think it would be a good idea for me to see you again," he replied, sounding bitter thinking about those dark and lonely times from which he had to extract himself.

"Not even as friends?" sounding disappointed but with a flare of flirtatious tone that she knew usually caused Kelsey to yield.

"Friends? My friends wouldn't have left me, Stephanie, especially when I needed them the most."

"—Fine, if that's the way you want it," Stephanie said sullenly and hung up the phone without saying goodbye.

Kelsey stared at the phone for a moment, then put it back in his pocket. He had always wondered how he would react once he heard from her again. He had wondered if Tai Chi was simply a form of escape from his true pain or if it had become an integral part of his being. As close as he had come to giving in, Kelsey was happy with his decision. He found joy in himself as he realized he had passed the test.

Kelsey's Journal: I thought the hole Stephanie left would never be repaired, that I would never feel like myself again. I was nearly destroyed. I can breathe now. I have moved on. My path is ever forward.

Joshua and Susan were having lunch together but Susan seemed preoccupied.

"Are you ok, Susan?" Joshua inquired.

"I'm fine," Susan replied instinctively.

"Are you sure? You seem a little distracted or something."

"Oh, don't mind me. So what do you think of Kelsey?" she changed the subject.

"I wasn't sure about him at first, but I think he'll bring positive changes to the organization," Joshua said.

They both agreed that although Kelsey didn't fit the typical corporate mold his unconventional methods somehow still worked.

After a brief silence, it became apparent to Joshua that Susan was truly struggling.

"Susan," Joshua leaned forward. "I can tell when something is wrong. What is going on?"

Tears slowly rolled down Susan's cheeks. Joshua leaned back, astonished. Tears were the last thing he ever expected to see from Susan, given the hard-nosed corporate persona she exemplified.

Joshua responded quietly. "Is it that bad?"

"I'm sorry," Susan reached for a napkin. "This is so embarrassing. Please excuse me." She stood to leave.

"No, wait," Joshua stood with her. "It's ok. Sit down. Let's talk about it."

Susan reluctantly sat back down.

"As a matter of fact, I'll tell you what," Joshua began. "Why don't you go to the restroom and get yourself together. We'll go back to work and then we can connect later for drinks. Does that sound ok?"

"This is so embarrassing," Susan buried her face in her hands.

"Susan, look at me," Joshua said.

Susan raised her head.

"You look awful," Joshua joked. "Black tears running down your face."

"That's not funny," Susan chuckled through her tears.

****

Susan barely noticed the homeless man who stood outside of her car window asking for money as she sat at a traffic light in downtown DC. She had just parted company with Joshua after sharing a few drinks at a bar. She was overwhelmed with embarrassment after having shared some personal struggles with him.

She cursed and motioned the homeless man away. "That damn liquor."

She recalled her conversation with Joshua.

****

"I feel like a failure," Susan said, defeated. "My employees are going behind my back complaining about changes I've made. I know what I'm doing. Everything I've done to this point has led me to where I am today. My education and over a decade of experience. I know everything I need to know and then some in my field. I have more knowledge and experience in my field than others who are 10 years my senior! "

"They could care less about your background, Susan," Joshua had said. "All they know is that you came in and disrupted their lives. It doesn't matter if you're trying to make things better. People don't like change. I guarantee you most of them have never heard of Sarbanes-Oxley, but they have heard of you. I'm dealing with a similar situation in my group. You know Greg? Well today, we had it out. Kelsey gave me some good advice and it worked for the most part. I still have to follow-up with Greg though, but I think everything went over well except the part where I told him he has to go back to school."

Susan cringed as she recalled the tears rolling down her cheeks again.

"Why do you let it get to you like this?" Joshua had asked. "When I leave work, I don't carry any of my work issues home. Don't you have a life?"

"That's just it," Susan had replied. "Look at me. Am I not attractive?"

"Of course you are."

"Then what's the problem? Why are all my weekends spent alone?"

Susan recalled Joshua's reaction. It had warmed her watching him drop his head.

So he does like me. It's just as Susan had thought.

****

Suddenly the blare of an automobile horn jolted Susan to the present. She was still in DC, sitting in traffic. She glanced to the left and noticed a familiar face: Kelsey. He rolled his window down after getting her attention.

"In the zone?" Kelsey inquired.

"I'm so sorry," she shouted back. "In DC you learn to shut out your surroundings while driving."

"So where are you headed?"

"Home. I live in Virginia."

"Do you have a few minutes?"

She had heard him but wasn't ready for that question. She needed time to respond.

"To talk," Kelsey continued. "Do you have a few minutes?"

The light had turned green and other horns were now blowing.

"Oh, sure," Susan finally answered. "Where do you have in mind?"

Susan read his lips as he said "follow me" and pulled away. She wondered what he wished to discuss as she hit the gas pedal.

CHAPTER 7

"I apologize if I've inconvenienced you," Kelsey began as he sat across from Susan stirring his tea.

"No, it's ok," Susan replied. "You probably saved me. I might have had one drink too many tonight. This cup of coffee is exactly what I needed. So where were you headed?"

"Actually, I was just riding." Kelsey replied as if he did not have a care in the world.

"Riding? 10:00 p.m.?"

"Yes. I worked in DC for years, but never realized how beautiful this city really is."

"Beautiful?" Susan asked, thinking to herself that his idea had never occurred to her before and looking at Kelsey as if he had two heads.

"Yes. Sometimes I'll just ride around in DC checking out the scenery, the night lights, the people, and everything else in and around it all."

"Well, ten hours per day of DC is about all I can handle," Susan said.

"So, let me ask you a question. Are you happy with your job?" Kelsey asked.

"Well, I'm not sure if I should be discussing my job right now. That's part of the problem. I bring my work home."

"Well, what about life after work?" Kelsey persisted.

"My, you're aggressive, aren't you?" Susan said, calling him on his intrusion.

"Yes, when there is something I want," Kelsey admitted.

"Well, what is it that you want?"

"What do I want?" Kelsey leaned forward. "I want to see you not only succeed in your professional life but your personal life as well. They are both intertwined you know.

When you separate your work life from your personal life, you never truly bring your entire person to bear on a problem or obstacle. Each one feeds the other, so whether you want to or not, you bring your issues from work home, and you take your personal issues to work."

"Oh really," Susan said. "Kelsey, every manual, teacher, or manager that I have worked for has told me exactly the opposite but now that you've got my attention, let me hear what you have to say."

"At my last corporate America job, I almost had a nervous breakdown," Kelsey revealed. "Not because of the pressure brought on by the position, but because of the pressure I put on myself. I had all these standards that I had set for myself, standards that were proven to work because I had used them to get where I was. I was a VP many years junior to my peers in that company with a six-figure salary."

"Six figures?" Susan nodded appreciatively.

"Yes, and one day, I just gave that up."

"You gave that up? Why?" Susan could not believe what she just heard.

"Well, when you arrive at higher corporate levels, it's easy to become arrogant, but my biggest problem was that I didn't want to lose what I had accomplished. I knew what it took to get there, and I knew what it took to stay there. I was determined not to fail."

"So what happened?" Susan asked, intrigued.

"The tighter I gripped and fought to maintain that same standard of excellence, the more elusive it became. I guess you can say that I lost the battle—both of holding on too tight, and the job itself—but overall I still feel I won the war. I hope what I am about to say does not confuse you. Before you can get strong, you have to become weak. I became very weak. I had come to a crossroad in my life, and I had to choose to continue the way I was and die of a heart attack or truly learn to live by doing things my way."

"You got weak?"

"Listen, Susan, how many hours of sleep do you get at night?"

"Five to six," she shrugged.

"And you wake up feeling refreshed, right?"

"Sometimes," she answered truthfully. She knew that there were more mornings she woke up wishing for a few more hours of respite.

"Well, there is more to you than just your body. You have an inner-self, an inner being that needs refreshing too." Kelsey continued.

"Do you sometime find yourself waking up in the morning and still very tired?"

Susan nodded in agreement.

"When it gets to the point that not even sleep is enough, it means your resources are running low. You are pushing your body to the limit. Something has got to give. You are getting very close to reaching that critical point where you will just break down. That's where I was."

Susan stared intently.

"People usually don't take their health seriously until after there has been some sort of traumatic event such as a heart attack, a stroke, or a nervous breakdown. Go online, do your research. Talk to your doctor. He'll tell you the same thing."

There was a moment of silence as Susan registered the information.

"It's easy to walk away from six figures when your life is at stake."

"Wow, was it that serious?" Susan asked with great interest.

"Yes. That's why I got into leadership consulting. I wanted to help people and have the flexibility to select my assignments so I could help those who needed it the most. I use Strategic Leadership Consultant services as a mechanism to enter a company. Once embedded, I do what I do best."

Kelsey continued. "At one point in my career, I ran from who I was. I hid behind a computer terminal as a small systems integrator so I would not have to interact with people. Let me tell you, that did not work for very long. Before I knew it, I had helped the company open three more locations and was running the main headquarters. No matter how much I tried to run away from what I was destined to do, I ended up where I was and I was so miserable. I remember calling my mentor from the military, a two-star general, and he flat out asked me, 'What are you doing, Kelsey? You have forgotten more about leadership than you will ever know about computers.'

"Now I have accepted who I am and embraced my fate in life. My mission is to help people become better professionals by helping people reconnect with their true aspirations and their true selves. Few understand, but most don't at first. Many people at first think my counsel is all crazy gibberish; but after some soul searching and really giving themselves a chance to look inward for the first time, they also discover what I have come to realize.

"Susan, if you want to know the truth, that is why I am here tonight; to help you reconnect with yourself to bring you back into balance."

"So how do I begin to connect?" Susan asked.

"First, go home and get some sleep," Kelsey instructed. Then first thing in the morning we'll begin by understanding what's going on in your department."

Kelsey's Journal: Susan will learn to rely on her personal strength, intuition, and her keen ability to identify problem areas, as well as opportunities. She will not be forced to rely on decoding vague inferences from Edward, or anyone else who withholds feedback as a power play.

Konrad reflected on the past month as he sat in his office. There were hints of light as the sun slowly made its debut for the morning. Reality Solutions' numbers hadn't changed on paper, but he had never been happier. He stopped going to a bar for days and even his usual serving of Scotch in the morning. He wondered if he should be more worried, but then he remembered something Kelsey had said: "Being worried has very little to do with results." Konrad was happy. He knew that by hiring Kelsey and making personal changes that would lead to making wise professional decisions, he was doing everything within his power to change his circumstances. The key to success was to fail, then try again, but not make the same mistake twice. And if it didn't work? No, it would work. He was really starting to believe Kelsey's quote:

"Failure is not an option! Sometimes you cannot rush a solution. Problems will resolve themselves in time, if you put the right people in place. You have got to trust your people or get rid of them. Your job is to create an environment for success. 'Build the box and let your people fill the box, then expand the box.'"

Konrad just surprised himself with another thought. He was so used to trying to control every aspect of his life, yet he was now beginning to differentiate between where his control started and stopped, and to maximize the former. His reaction first confused him but Konrad realized how liberating it was. He began to relax and let go of his tension, and believe that his personal transformation ran deeper than he realized. The change was beginning to stick. He stretched his arms out feeling happy and satisfied with himself.

Konrad scrolled through his emails and stopped on one he had received from Edward. Apparently it had been sent at 11:53 pm last night. He just knew that it was not going to be a pleasant topic and frowned even without realizing it.

It read:

Konrad,

I would like to meet with you first thing in the morning regarding Kelsey Knowles. I feel that we have been flexible and have cooperated with him but there still haven't been any positive results. I would like to discuss other options.

Edward

"He just won't quit," Konrad muttered, feeling a burst of irritation.

****

Edward entered Konrad's office with two binders. Apparently he had put a lot of effort into his rebuttal. Konrad could not help but wonder if Edward's motives were to get rid of Kelsey rather than to help the company.

"Thanks for your time," Edward said as he sat down and handed Konrad a binder. "I've put together a plan."

"Wait a minute," Konrad interrupted. "Let's discuss Kelsey first. What are your concerns?"

"Look, Konrad," Edward began, "the bottom line is results. There has been no improvement in our numbers since he's been here. This is nothing personal against him. I think he's a good guy with some bright ideas, but this touchy feely stuff just isn't working. The bottom line is, unless we make some changes to the bottom line, people are going to be out of jobs."

"I am well aware of the seriousness of our situation." Konrad sat back in his chair. "We didn't get into this situation overnight, and we're not going to come out of it overnight. One thing that I have learned already from my association with Kelsey is that Reality Solutions does not have one big problem but rather a series of little problems that have been ignored, slowly bleeding into one another and before we knew it, we faced a crisis that seems insurmountable."

"I'm aware of that, Konrad," Edward said dismissively, "but if you would take a look at this proposal, I'm sure you'll like it."

Konrad recalled all the times Edward had strong-armed him in the past with his proposals. Konrad's first reaction was to reject Edward's proposal, but he hesitated. Edward was an intelligent man, and perhaps the recent circumstances had forced him to create something useful.

After a brief pause, Konrad gave explicit instructions to Edward. "Kelsey and I are meeting this afternoon for a progress report. I'll review your proposal and have a decision to you by tomorrow. Edward, I want you to remember a quote that Kelsey gave me the other day by Terry Goodkind, 'It is the weight of one snowflake that causes an avalanche.' If you were so aware of Reality Solutions' demise, where was your advice earlier before the avalanche hit? Why did you wait until now? I will review your proposal and get back to you."

Edward agreed reluctantly.

****

"Phase One is complete," Kelsey said as he handed Konrad a report. "Starting this week I will begin Phase Two during which I will deal more directly with internal conflicts within individual departments. I will use this phase to challenge norms, to question formal and informal processes, and to force your staff to think outside of traditional boundaries. This phase will be the most difficult of all. Some people will immediately grasp what I am doing and embrace the change and others will retreat back into the safe confines of the norm. Others may even attempt to sabotage the changes you wish to make."

Konrad skimmed over the report.

"Can you give me a timeframe of how long this phase will take?"

"You should see changes within the next month." Kelsey replied. "I've gained the confidence and trust of most all your staff members, and I think they will listen to me."

"So, Kelsey, what is your overall opinion?" Konrad leaned forward in his chair.

"My overall opinion?"

"Yes. What do you think about my people?"

"You've got a good group. Some of them are set in their ways, but they're too concerned about their jobs to truly speak their minds. You have a few rising stars as well. Joshua Brown and Susan Lockhart stand out. I believe they will help your company grow."

Konrad agreed and reiterated his support of Kelsey during the coming months.

"OK." Kelsey stood to exit. "I guess I better get to work."

****

Joshua was organizing his desk when Susan knocked, then peered from behind his office door.

"Good morning," she offered.

"Good morning, Susan. Come in."

"Are you sure?"

Joshua noticed how bright and refreshed Susan appeared.

"You look," Joshua searched for the right words, "alive."

Susan smiled as she sat down.

"So am I missing something here?" Joshua leaned back in his chair.

"Excuse me?" Susan blushed.

"Something's going on."

"Well, after you and I parted last night, I ran into Kelsey."

"Kelsey Knowles?"

"Yes, and we had a cup of coffee together."

"Last night? I thought he was smooth but he is quick too," Joshua teased.

"No, it's not like that." Susan shook her head and waved her hand in dismissing Joshua's comment. With a more serious tone, she continued. "We just happened to bump into each other on my way home and I guess by looking at my face, he knew something was not right.

He offered to buy me a cup of coffee. I was hesitant but I say what the hell, it's not like I had to rush home."

"Anyhow, we were talking about work and he was genuine and made me feel very comfortable. We talked about things that made a lot of sense and made me think about some things. Things I have never given much thought, or maybe I did. I did not realize that some of these things were always hovering over my head. I never had time to think about it. Anyhow, it was an eye opener and when I went home, I started reading his book. I can't say that I fully understand some of the concepts and, to be truthful, I don't entirely agree that all his concepts belong in the business setting, but he made enough of an impression that I am willing to give it a try."

Joshua concurred. "I guess I can see what you mean. He did offer me a solution to my problem with Greg, and I think it might work."

"Exactly. Everything is so much clearer. It's like I'm seeing this person in the mirror and wondering where have you been? Have I truly existed? Have you read the book?"

"I've started it. It's about work-life balance, which I've heard about from more corporate seminars than I can count, but there's something deeper and different. I'll keep you posted as I keep reading."

"So what do you think about the book so far?"

"Better than I thought. A little left field but certainly an eye opener."

"I'm definitely going to finish it. Well, anyway, I wanted to thank you for tolerating me yesterday evening. I know my company wasn't the best but thanks for hanging in there. I didn't get you in trouble with your girlfriend, did I?"

"And if you did? It's not like I can come sleep over your place."

"Well, I guess that's something we'll never know," Susan flirted as she opened the door and left.

****

Kelsey was sitting in the conference room preparing his notes when Joshua entered for their next meeting.

"Hello, Joshua. Come right in."

"Hello, Kelsey."

"Now let me make sure I understand, you run the Product Department, but Customer Service also reports into you. The customer service group is the primary conduit for your customers to place orders. So once a client is secured by a sales representative, they are turned over to your department, right?"

"Yes. We take their orders and also deal with any complaints. More importantly, we also try to increase our sales by keeping customers informed of any changes in our processes."

"So how much do you know about your clients?" Kelsey asked.

"What do you mean?" Joshua answered, puzzled.

"Do you have any additional data about your customers or things that can help you to understand more about your clients and establish and strengthen your relationships with them?"

"No. I can't say that we do."

"Tell me about your department. What is the average length of time the employees have been in your department?"

"I'd say three to five years."

Kelsey took his time to process the information and let the answers flow.

"First, how do you know that your customers are happy with your service?"

"You know what, I don't know," Joshua replied. "I never thought about it. I guess it might be a good idea to find out."

"Exactly. You can't fix what you don't know is broken," Kelsey stated.

"I suggest you create a survey to submit to each of your customers. Find out any complaints they have and ways they think your service can be improved.

Whether you're able to satisfy every comp irrelevant; what's important is that you show them you care. Securing a client is hard, but retaining that client is twice as hard. Also remember, once you take a customer's feedback you need to develop a process that shows the customer you are taking action to improve. Remember that quick hitters can instantly increase motivation both internally and externally. Everyone likes to think they add value." Kelsey stopped just long enough to make sure that Joshua was processing what he had said so far.

"Next, three years is too long for any employee to stay in your department. It's hard enough to stay motivated after two years of filling client orders and addressing complaints. Employees should be recycled into the company to keep fresh and motivated people dealing with your customers. This way, your employees don't become too comfortable with your clients. You know how it is when you get comfortable around your significant other. You do and say things that you'd never have done or say when you first met. It's the same in business, except we can't afford to make the same mistakes in the business field. The consequences can be detrimental."

"It makes sense," Joshua nodded with approval. He was amazed at how Kelsey's solutions were so obvious. He wondered why he hadn't thought of these options himself. Then he recalled Susan's earlier statement, "This man is phenomenal—with his insight and his depth." Joshua resolved that he would complete Kelsey's book that night.

"So did you think about what I said before regarding your employee?" Kelsey inquired.

"Employee?" Joshua frowned. "Oh yes, Greg. I promoted him to an Assistant Director position several days ago with a raise after the probation period. He looked surprised but I think, overall, it went well."

"Good," said Kelsey with approval. Let's get together again same time next week to evaluate your progress."

Joshua agreed and extended his hand.

"Kelsey, is there any way we can meet off-line? I would appreciate your insight on a few issues if you're not too busy."

"Sure," Kelsey answered with sincerity.

"Great. Here is my cell phone number." Joshua wrote down his cell phone number on the back of his business card and handed it to Kelsey.

"Please call me and let me know when you might be available. Thank you, Kelsey."

Kelsey's Journal: Joshua is beginning to realize that he cannot force situations and expect his pre-determined, logical result. He must learn to walk in the shoes of his employees and transcend his youth and precocity. He must balance humility with unwavering leadership. As he matures, his emotions will also be more in check; his responses will be deliberate and mindful.

CHAPTER 8

Kelsey knocked on Susan's office door and entered after he heard a faint "Come in."

"How are you doing, Susan?"

"Good. I guess. As you can see, I am swamped over here."

"Yes, I figured. I was waiting 15 minutes in the conference room for you."

"Oh, no!" Susan exclaimed. "I am so sorry. I completely forgot."

"It's ok," Kelsey assured her. "It happens to all of us."

"No, really. I normally never miss a meeting. This is so unlike me," Susan said, flustered.

"Is it ok if we meet here instead?" Kelsey asked.

"Are you sure?"

"Oh yeah, not a problem—as long as it's not inconveniencing you too much."

"No, not at all, thank you, Kelsey. I really appreciate it."

Kelsey sat back and pulled his notepad from his briefcase.

"So tell me, Susan," he began. "What's a day like from sun-up to sun-down for the Director of the Finance Department at Reality Solutions?" Kelsey asked thoughtfully.

"Well, I spend the first hour going through emails, which usually turns into two hours," she answered with a sigh. Then I hold a staff meeting for an hour every morning at 10 to assess the progress from the previous day. The rest of day just dissolves between emails, meetings, phone calls, crisis from past management and fixing what previous managements failed to do. Before I know it, it's already 5:30 or 6:00

p.m. and I have more on my plate than when I came to work that morning. I feel like a hamster stuck on a wheel and getting nowhere." Susan felt herself getting frustrated at just the thought of it all and the weight on her shoulders seemed to feel heavier by the minute.

She continued. "We're currently about two months behind on a complete report of this past fiscal year's totals. That's a big problem because we can't adequately predict the next fiscal year's projected totals. The previous director did not keep sufficient records of the financial transactions with many of our customers, so I've got my work cut out for me for the next few months."

"So how do you plan to catch up?"

Susan paused for a moment.

"Well, I would love to hire some temporary help, but I know that it's not in the budget. I guess I'm going to have to ask some employees to work overtime. I don't think Edward will approve it but I don't see any other way at this point."

"How much time do you spend going through emails each day?" Kelsey queried.

"I'll say a minimum of at least three hours a day," Susan shrugged.

"How essential is each email you read?" Kelsey asked.

"Well, not all of them are essential," Susan admitted. "Actually, the majority of them are copies. My employees 'cc' emails to me to keep me abreast of what's going on."

"So you spend a majority of three hours reading 'cc' copies of emails from your employees helping you stay informed, and then hold a staff meeting for an hour a day to stay updated?"

"That seems about right," Susan agreed.

"You don't see anything wrong with that?" Kelsey probed.

"No, not really. I'm very organized and very detailed. That is necessary, especially when dealing with money."

"I agree, but I have another question. Do you trust your employees?" Kelsey asked.

"Trust them how? Trust them as in misappropriating funds?"

"No, I mean their skills."

Susan thought for a moment.

"Yes, I do. I have some very capable employees."

"Then why do you feel the need to stay abreast of every minute detail?" Kelsey asked.

"Because it is my job to keep an eye on my employees and know what is going on in my own department. Isn't that what I am supposed to do? If something goes wrong, I'll need to know what is going on so that I can explain it to upper management."

"But don't you agree that something is going to have to give? You're already behind, so you're going to have to sacrifice something. You spend 15 hours a week reading and organizing emails and another 5 hours in staff meetings. That's a total of 20 hours that could be used more effectively in other areas," Kelsey advised.

"What other choices do I have? It's just a part of the job. If you have any better ideas, I'd like to hear them." Susan was aggravated that Kelsey was questioning her methods and her management skills. She felt that he was attacking her ability and the skills she perfected over the years. She could not help but feel defensive, but decided to keep her cool.

"Well, first of all, instead of reading each email, just file it and only read the important ones. You could either spend your evenings at home reading through them, or task someone else in your department with that responsibility. As far as those staff meetings, once a week should suffice. You're going to have to learn to trust that your employees are capable enough to complete their responsibilities. If they are not capable, then you have another issue."

Susan was hesitant, but she nodded as she digested the information.

"So what initial suggestions would you have to catch up without costing the company more money?" Susan asked.

"Assess the workload of your employees. Who is the most and least busy? Start delegating responsibilities according to their workloads and ability to complete the task at hand satisfactorily."

Susan nodded with approval.

"Susan, why do you feel the need to micro-manage?"

Susan thought for a moment then replied, "Because I feel that a good manager should know what is going on in his or her own department. Well, I guess ultimately, fear of failure."

Kelsey nodded and then replied, "I'm going to let you in on a secret." He leaned forward. "Mistakes are inevitable. Don't resist them. All you can do is be as prepared as you can when you make them. Don't be afraid to take risks. Show me someone who has never failed and I will show you someone who has never taken any risks. From my point of view, the most successful people are the ones that have failed and learned from their mistakes and yet never make the same mistake twice."

He smiled with an air of a wise teacher looking at his pupil.

"The gospel according to St. Kelsey," Susan joked.

"I have one more question, Susan."

"Can you describe to me the strategy that you want to implement in your department on one page?"

"What?" Susan exclaimed. "No way. There is so much ground to cover."

"Therein lies part of your problem," Kelsey advised.

"What do you mean?"

"Apparently, you're not clear on what your goal is; therefore, how do you expect your department to be clear?"

"Of course I am clear on what my goal is," Susan protested.

"Then you should be able to describe your goal clearly on one sheet of paper. Not in detail but at least a concise overview. And most importantly, your team ıould be able to immediately repeat your shared goal asked individually or as part of a group."

"A consultant I once worked with was fond of pointing out, 'The results of planning should be clarity of thought.' If you cannot lay out your strategy on one sheet of paper then the strategy is not clear to you."

Susan pondered Kelsey's comment.

Kelsey pressed on. "Remember what you told me regarding improving upon corporate management techniques?" Susan replied that she did, in fact, remember.

"So have you thought on how to implement your new strategy?"

"No, I've actually been too busy to think about it," Susan admitted.

Kelsey shook his head. "So you're overwhelmed with work but none of it includes some of the key goals you mentioned to me earlier?"

Susan sighed as the impact of Kelsey's words sunk in.

"It's ok, Susan. Time management and execution are central themes that keep cropping up in most corporations. Most leaders are unable to convert strategy into an executable plan. More importantly, even when a plan is presented, the leaders fail to align incentives so people will be motivated to change."

At that moment, Susan's respect for Kelsey was solidified. Before this conversation and despite her increasing admiration of Kelsey, she still slightly questioned whether he was legitimate and was subconsciously waiting for his flaws to be exposed. She was more of a learner than director in his presence, an indulgence she hadn't realized she missed after all these years of leading teams and being responsible for the development of others. With all of her education and experience, she still was at a loss as to how Kelsey made things sound so simple.

"Let's meet tomorrow to discuss this further," Kelsey said sensing her vulnerability.

Susan nodded and stared at the door after he left.

****

Kelsey recalled the day's events as he returned home that evening. As Kelsey was driving and listening to his Tai Chi music, he took the opportunity to conduct his breathing exercises. Inhale five seconds, hold for five seconds, exhale for five seconds. Four breaths a minute, he recalled Sifu teaching:

"Chi energy is not a mystery. The earth is full of electromagnetic energy. The earth's poles constantly release energy, which ionizes the air. The deeper you breathe, the more energy you bring into the body. This energy revitalizes you. But pollution, smog, and vehicle exhaust block the intake of these healing energies. As you become more advanced in Tai Chi, I will then start teaching you how to use the healing breath to take Tai Chi to the next level."

Kelsey reveled in his sense of accomplishment. The benefits of being in harmony and in balance never ceased to amaze him. He recalled how easily answers came to him as he met with each department head. He remembered the look of hesitance and amazement that each of his clients held, but also realized that his toughest challenges lay ahead. He had to get the management of Reality Solutions to a point where they could experience a sense of balance and clarity, and their own personal enlightenment for themselves, so that they could produce the necessary answers in any given situation.

****

Konrad knocked on Edward's office door before entering.

"Good morning, Konrad."

"Good morning, Edward."

"Thanks for stopping by."

"No problem," Konrad said as he sat down. "I've reviewed your proposal, and I like it."

Edward smiled, satisfied.

"However, I want to hold off a bit more. I want to give Kelsey another month. I believe he has a lot to offer our management staff. If after a month things haven't changed, I'd like to look at your proposal with the staff. Besides, part of bringing in Kelsey was under the condition that I give him uninterrupted and undivided support without expecting instant results and the agreement was that I give him at least three months before we can expect to see any improvement. I did not expect an instant fix or our numbers to climb right away. I do however see that people are more motivated and have positive energy to those I spoke with."

Edward did not like what he was hearing but agreed reluctantly. He was more convinced than ever that Konrad had not been the same lately. The Konrad he had known for the last 10 years was nowhere to be found, and Edward feared he might be losing the unchallenged and unfettered CEO-level influence he had long enjoyed and felt entitled to receive. Displeased, Edward had had enough.

"By the way, Edward," Konrad said as he stood up. "Have you read Kelsey's book?"

"I can't say that I have."

"You really should read it," Kelsey said.

"I'll take a look at it," Edward replied half-heartedly.

"Edward, I know you don't appreciate what I am doing here with Kelsey, but I truly feel this is what the company needs right now. One particular quote in Kelsey's book stands out for me: 'Leadership is to compete for people's hearts, something that is only possible if those at the helm are committed to delivering the truth. Nothing destroys the leader's sense of purpose – and with it the respect and trust of those around him/her – more dramatically than half-truths, self-serving statements and the belief that people are easier to control if they don't know what's going on. Quoted by John O. Burdett.'"

"As leaders of this company, we both need to do some soul searching about our actions over the past few years and be clear about the parts we have played that brought our company to the brink of the abyss. Do yourself a favor and read the book, Edward," Konrad said as he left.

****

As Joshua browsed his emails, he noticed something that disturbed him. Three of his top employees sent emails to Greg and a "cc" to Joshua notifying him that they were taking personal leaves all on the same day. Alarmed, Joshua called Greg to come into his office immediately.

"Hello, Joshua," Greg said as he entered.

"Hi, Greg," Joshua began. "Are you aware that Patricia, Steve and Lawrence are all taking off the same day next week?"

"Yes," Greg replied. "They requested Friday off last week."

"And you didn't check with me?"

"I'm sorry; I did not know I had to check with you first. Are you saying I don't have the authority to make that type of decision?" Greg retorted.

"That's not the point. I need to be apprised of issues relating to insufficient coverage," said Joshua.

"So what's the point of being the Assistant Director if I need to check with you every time a decision needs to be made?"

"You're missing the point, Greg. You don't see the big picture."

"Yes, I do see the big picture. You thought that by making me the Assistant Director you would shut me up, but I'm no fool. I know what's going on."

"What are you talking about?"

Greg looked away as he stood up.

"Greg, you really should calm down and let me explain. Would you sit down please?"

Greg sat back down without making eye contact with Joshua.

"As I advised in our department meeting, we are about to undergo a reassessment evaluation. This is based upon the recommendation of a consultant that our president hired. I've got to know the status of each individual employee over the next two weeks. Not to mention that now is crunch time, and I never would have approved allowing three of our best employees to be off on the same day."

Greg began to understand his error in judgment.

"This is not about whether you have the authority to make the decision, but whether the decision was a good decision to begin with," Joshua said.

"My apologies," Greg offered. "I'll make sure it doesn't happen again."

Joshua nodded, trying to look calm but unable to completely control his frustration. Inwardly Joshua was questioning the logic of promoting Greg, but the decision was made and it was the right decision.

****

Joshua finished his third bottle of beer as he watched the basketball game. For the first time he was starting to feel worried about his job. Could he turn things around? Was promoting Greg a mistake? Would Greg eventually undermine him and turn all his employees against him?

Joshua remembered Kelsey's consultation: "The leader's job is to create an environment for success. Create the box. Your employees need to be able to make mistakes—controlled mistakes—so they can learn and grow. If you interfere or crush them and don't give proper guidance then they will never mature to fill the box and you will demolish future chances to expand the box."

What are you doing, Joshua? He thought to himself. *This isn't like you. You are home now, not at work. Forget about work and stop stressing. Just enjoy the game!*

Joshua attempted to focus on the game but his mind slipped right back to his worries. Before Konrad hired Kelsey as a consultant, Joshua wasn't fully aware of his own circumstances, but his conversations with Kelsey had changed his perspective. He was glad to have more insight, but with more insight came a heightened awareness of the weaknesses in his department. Joshua popped the top of another beer.

"Why couldn't I see the solutions?" he thought. Then he recalled one of the lines he read in Kelsey's book: "Simplicity can be evasive." Suddenly his cell phone rang. It was Kelsey.

"Thanks for calling," Joshua replied as he sat up.

"How're you doing?" Kelsey responded with genuine concern. Is this a good time?"

"Yes, I was just watching the game, but nothing good is on anyhow."

"Well, you said you wanted to talk about a few things, so I figured I'd give you a call."

"Your timing is perfect."

"Good. Good. So what's on your mind?"

"Honestly. How did you come up with those solutions so easily? I'm mad at myself for not seeing them sooner. They were so simple."

Kelsey smiled. He had wondered how he would introduce his techniques. He didn't know it would be as simple as answering a question.

"For me it's Tai Chi."

"What?"

"It's an Asian form of therapy that promotes health and mental balance."

"Like a religion?" Joshua asked.

"Not even. It's basically a workout that enhances your health and mental awareness. It teaches you to achieve mental clarity through the use of active meditation. By seeing through the fog of uncertainty, it allows you to unite more readily with your subconscious, thereby making answers easier to come by.

"As I told Susan the other day, the result of planning should be clarity of thought. What I haven't told Susan yet is that clarity is a hard skill to master. If you can ask the question, then you are ready for the answer," Kelsey continued. "Most people try to separate their personal lives from their professional lives; this in and of itself leads to internal conflict. What society has been teaching people all these years is to develop psychosomatic disorders. Before you can readily access your subconscious, you first must accept who you are."

"What does working out have to do with finding answers?"

"It's not your typical workout, such as free weights or nautilus. It's a series of concentrated movements founded in martial arts techniques."

Joshua nodded. "My nephew takes martial arts classes now, and they promote mental discipline."

"Yes," Kelsey agreed, "but Tai Chi is not quite as focused on the martial arts aspects as it is connecting the different aspects of yourself: mentally, physically, and spiritually."

"Spiritually?"

"Yes, spiritually." Kelsey laughed, accustomed to that kind of reaction when he mentioned the word "spirituality." "But not in the traditional sense."

"Do you mean God?" Joshua asked, wary of religion in a work setting.

"Well, I guess you can call him God, another religion calls him Buddha and someone else calls him Jehovah, Mohammad, the list goes on. Regardless, the key is tapping into the source of what brings one peace. Spirituality for one could be planting trees, meditation or praying."

"Interesting. So how would I get started?"

"Why don't you join me in my next workout?"

"Ok. I think I'll do that."

Kelsey's Journal: There is an Asian – Ashram, Yoga, Buddha or Hindi belief or philosophy that everyone is born with all the answers to one's own questions. We just need to learn to listen to our inner self and find the answers that are already there.

CHAPTER 9

Susan sipped on her soda while sitting at a table outside of the restaurant where she had just finished lunch. She was preparing to leave when a man slightly older than she approached her.

"Do you mind if I sit down?"

Susan was intrigued. He appeared to embody the complete package: tall, handsome, well-groomed and well-dressed.

"It's so crowded around here; it's hard to find somewhere to sit," the stranger said.

Internally, Susan warmed at the tone of his voice.

"I don't mind," she replied. "Actually, I was just finishing."

"That's too bad."

"Why?" Susan replied, obviously flattered but trying to contain her interest.

Susan paused. She couldn't believe how forward he was, but at the same time, seemingly respectful and kind. She even wondered if she should be concerned.

The man, sensing her nervousness, quickly replied, "I'm Jason Wainwright, and I've noticed you here several times. I'm a bit shy, and I've been hoping for the right opportunity to meet you."

"It's ok," Susan smiled. "Sure, I can take a few more minutes."

As they talked, Susan found herself willing to give Jason more of her time. It was as if two conversations were going on simultaneously: one with Jason and one in her mind as she recalled certain quotes in Kelsey's book, which alluded to success in all areas of one's life. Suddenly she realized an hour had passed.

"Oh, my!" She stood up, glancing at her watch. "I didn't realize this much time had passed.

"I'm sorry," Jason replied. "That was selfish of me to take up your entire lunchtime."

"No, it's fine. I enjoyed our conversation," she said.

"May I call you?" Jason asked.

"Sure," Susan smiled.

They exchanged business cards as she reluctantly hurried off. As Susan rushed back to her office building, she knew that everything was connected. She had already begun to implement Kelsey's suggestions. There seemed to be a new energy in her department. Then she recalled one of the statements from Kelsey's book: "Help from outside is nothing unless help is matched from within."

Now Susan had met Jason, someone who had been admiring her for awhile, waiting for the right opportunity to meet her. She recalled how she almost bypassed the restaurant today where she met Jason because it was crowded. The last few weeks had been very fulfilling for Susan. She had decided to implement suggestions from her sessions with Kelsey. Instead of pushing her strategy, which even Kelsey agreed was sound, how about letting her staff own the creation and implementation of the department's new strategy?

Susan recalls firing back, "What are you talking about!? There is no way I can let someone else implement this project. It would fail."

Kelsey calmly stated the obvious, "And that is the point. By giving up control and empowering others, you will actually gain more control and create buy-in for this new initiative."

Kelsey continued. "It is obvious that no one knows this project like you do. If you give it away, people will be forced to engage you to ensure they do not fail. Nobody comes into work and decides, 'I want to be a failure today.' Most people try to do the right thing. hange Leadership is the hardest part of any project. ople are comfortable doing what they know. That is why it typically takes years for those large scale ERP projects ever to recoup their investment. Everyone wants to focus on the technology process and fails to address the people factor."

"As the Project Leader, you need to set up a structure that ensures your success. Create a Sub-Project Leader, a Process Sub-Project Leader, and you manage the overall project. Your job is to manage stakeholder expectations. I guarantee you that managing stakeholders will be the hardest thing you have ever done. Remember to create an environment where you manage the Sub-Project Leaders at the milestone level. Do not, I repeat, do not micro-manage against a Project Software management program," Kelsey advised.

"You also need to create an Approval Committee to ensure that you have the right level of support in the organization to obliterate political or cultural barriers within the organization."

Susan recollected how she had questioned Kelsey on this point, "If I create an Executive Committee, nothing will ever get done. Those groups never make decisions."

Kelsey smiled with the wisdom of an experienced warrior with an old scar, "And whose fault is that?"

Susan just stared at Kelsey and finally answered, "It is their fault. They are paid the big bucks to make decisions."

"Wrong answer, Susan."

"As a director in any organization, your job is to recommend strategy for approval and implement approved strategies. Executives should either approve or disapprove a strategy. One of the things that I have noticed is that the higher individuals move up in an organization, the more they are afraid to take risks. Once they reach that comfort zone, they no longer take the risks and become commonplace in the execution of their jobs. They start fearing the loss of prestige, power, wealth, and security that they have worked so hard to obtain."

Kelsey continued. "Decisions are dragged out to ensure that every conceivable issue is addressed. By that time, you have a strategy that is no longer addressing the immediate needs of an organization. As an Airborne Ranger Infantryman, we had a saying, 'It is better to execute an 80% plan violently on time than to execute a 100% plan late. Executing a plan late will get people killed versus executing on time and trusting that you have trained your people sufficiently to accomplish the mission.' The same is true in Corporate America. If it takes one year to develop the strategy there is a good chance the competitive landscape has changed. So, Susan, why do you think Senior Executives are afraid to take risk?"

By this point, Susan had learned not to answer rhetorical questions.

"It's about managing risk. How do you spread the risk around among senior executives that they are comfortable saying yes? When you structure your Approval Committee, first be cognizant of the name. The name of the committee immediately implies you want action on behalf of the members. Select a cross functional representation of executives high enough up that can make decisions. Do not select an even number just in case opinions are split evenly; three or five member committees are ideal.

"Here is the dilemma that you will have to face: Are you comfortable enough with yourself to take personal risk to include possible termination for a strategy that you recommend? You have to be willing to present a recommended strategy to the Approval Committee and structure it such that they agree. If the strategy fails, you have to be willing to assume the consequences of failure. You have to present your strategy is such a way that the Approval Committee will either say 'Yes' or 'No.' This is the crux of what I call 'Decisive Leadership.' Once you win 'Yes,' you now have the authority to eliminate any resistance. If you set up your communications properly, how many people will tell ou no when three of the top vice-presidents have ready said yes?"

Susan remembered marveling at the simplicity of Kelsey's coaching. She was so encouraged and enthusiastic; she could not wait to get started.

With the Decisive Leadership knowledge and understanding, Susan smiled as she remembered Kelsey calling it enlightenment. Susan had immediately started seeing positive changes as she instituted her strategies. She was more energetic than she'd been in years. Even her personal life seemed to be taking an upward turn.

****

Joshua had just finished an hour-long Tai Chi workout with Kelsey in the park. He had been working out with Kelsey resolutely for the past two weeks. Kelsey insisted that they work out away from the office. When he first started working out, Joshua was surprised to find that he was sweating from what seemed like such slow and effortless movements.

Joshua recalled his initial observation about the workouts, "When we first began, I had no idea it would be this hard. All you ever see is advertisements for older people to take up Tai Chi or a group of older Asians doing Tai Chi in the park. I never knew it could be this hard."

"Joshua, Tai Chi, loosely translated, means Grand Ultimate. Once mastered, a Tai Chi practitioner can defend and defeat just about any assailant. Tai Chi is about balance. Think of water. It is very soft, but water is also one of the most destructive force on this planet. Tai Chi is foremost a Martial Art. One of the side benefits of Tai Chi is the restorative nature it has on one's health. The movements are natural and designed to create balance."

"Tai Chi is a form of active meditation that facilitates the circulation of your Chi throughout the body. Chi is known as a body's energy source and channels. Through proper circulation of Chi, one will live longer through the proper management of stress and will help stave off illness. Asian medicine is designed around this principle. Asian medicine diagnoses blockages of the Chi and internally treats the blockage."

"One of the best known treatments is acupuncture. Acupuncture is designed to unblock the Chi to restore proper circulation. If one is stressed at work, his muscles become knotted. Most Americans simply seek a massage to treat tense muscles, but massages are only a temporary fix. Over time, this collection of stress throughout the body, which blocks the proper flow of Chi, leads to sickness such as heart attacks, strokes, cancer, and eventually death."

"Over time, with the continued practice of Tai Chi, you will notice old aches and pains will disappear. You will rarely catch colds, and a great side benefit is that you will excel at work. Tai Chi will help you focus mentally; through that focus you will be able to see a strategy from start to finish and reasonably predict the outcome. This will allow you to plan for those unexpected pitfalls that would have caused the strategy to fail previously."

****

Joshua felt confident as he drove to work the next morning. Things were falling in place, almost too easily. But something continued to nag, a feeling of uneasiness so subtle he could barely notice it, but it was there. He ignored it the warning and assumed he was being paranoid. He resolved to relax and enjoy the good fortune life had afforded him thus far.

When he arrived at work, there was a note on his desk. It read, "Joshua, come and see me ASAP... Konrad." Joshua was alarmed. Never, in the past, had Konrad left a note like this. Generally, Konrad sent an email or a voicemail, but never a handwritten note.

"Good morning," Konrad greeted Joshua as he entered his office.

"Good morning, Konrad. I received your note."

Konrad nodded. "It appears we may have a slight problem."

"A problem?" Joshua leaned forward.

"This morning I had several voicemails from clients. They were complaining about a survey form that was sent yesterday."

"A survey form?" Joshua frowned.

"You mean you weren't aware of it?" Konrad leaned forward.

Joshua paused. He recalled the survey form that he and Greg had been preparing to send to all clients. The survey was intended to serve a dual purpose: strengthen relationships with customers and determine weaknesses in their division. Apparently, Greg had moved forward with this project without getting Joshua's final approval. Now Joshua had a choice: hang Greg out to dry or protect him. For the sake of his own image, Joshua decided to cover for Greg and then deal with him later.

"Actually, I am," Joshua conceded.

"You mean you sent out a survey form to all of our customers without notifying me first?"

"Well, actually, it was an idea that Greg and I had been developing, but apparently there was a miscommunication on how to proceed with it. I take the responsibility, and I promise to handle it right away."

Joshua made a mental note that he still had a lot more work to do with Greg. He had to make Greg understand the bigger picture. What was it that Kelsey had said? "Sometimes knowing when not to fight is just as important as knowing how to fight. Everything has its proper place. When you try to manipulate a situation sometimes things will backfire on you and a good strategy will fail because you forced it."

Joshua refocused his attention back to Konrad.

"I am told that some of the questions concerned our customers' personal information. Is it true that we were requesting birthdays and wedding anniversary dates in this form?"

Konrad read over the rest of the form. Joshua tried hard to maintain his composure as the sudden fear of being fired raged within him and without even realizing it, he started slowing his breathing the way Kelsey had taught him. Four breaths a minute; inhale rejuvenating energy; exhale the stress. Learn not to panic. Learn to embrace those moments of adversity and wait for the right moment to grasp victory from the jaws of defeat.

After what seemed an eternity, Konrad made eye contact with Joshua. Joshua met his stare. If he was going to be fired, he'd take it like a man, not with his head hung low.

"Joshua," Konrad said firmly, "Nothing like this can ever happen again without me knowing about it. If so, there will be consequences. Understood?"

"Understood," Joshua nodded.

There was a moment of silence, and then Joshua stood to leave. As he started for the door, Konrad spoke.

"Off the record, I like the idea. Develop it some more and let me take a look at it."

Joshua was relieved. He had survived. What did Kelsey say? "That which does not kill us makes us stronger. The part that everyone always leaves out is that it hurts like hell until we get stronger." Joshua smiled again at that memory.

"Will do, and my most sincere apologies for the disturbance and confusion."

****

Within a few minutes of Joshua's leaving Konrad's office, Edward burst in.

"Now this is getting out of hand, Konrad."

Edward was holding up printed emails of the complaints he had received.

"Calm down, Edward."

"Calm down? We are trying to raise our numbers, and then this? I know who is behind this. It's that Kelsey character. He's giving our department heads a false sense of confidence and now it's affecting their work. I tell you if you don't get this thing under control, he's going to be the downfall of our company."

"Edward, please calm down and have a seat."

Edward took a couple of deep breaths then sat down.

"Konrad," Edward began, "I have been trying to be patient with this idea. You know I never agreed from the beginning, but I have been patient, and now you can see firsthand why I never agreed."

Edward sat back with a slight air of confidence. He knew Konrad was cornered. Now he'd be forced to look at things from his point of view.

"I agree," Konrad began. "What Joshua did was a mistake... or just a naïve misstep by not getting our approval first. Did you even read the survey form, yet?"

"No," Edward was taken back by the question.

"It's actually a pretty good survey. It needs some work but overall it was good and I can actually see how it can strengthen our relationship with our clients once it has been tweaked a little. Let's put this in perspective. Out of 200 plus customers, we only received three complaints. That's really not bad."

"So what are you saying?" Edward blurted as he saw his advantage slowly slipping away.

"I'm saying that I believe Kelsey's techniques are encouraging our managers to think outside the box. The risk we run is keeping them under control, but I'd rather have that problem than having managers twiddling their thumbs."

Edward was silent. He began to shake his head, then stood and stared accusingly at Konrad. "You know, Konrad," he began. "I'm really not sure how much more of this I can take."

Then Edward turned and left.

****

Kelsey scanned Susan's notes as they sat in the conference room. He wanted to ensure she was prepared to present her strategy to the VPs of Finance, Senior VPs of Finance, and Chief Financial Officer.

"Did you explore every possibility, every possible question they can ask that will divert from your goal?"

"Yes, I did," Susan replied.

"Remember, you want to leave with a yes approval of your strategy; but just in case you get a no, it should be with an explanation that will ultimately give you a yes. This is the essence of Decisive Leadership."

Kelsey continued reading her draft.

"This looks good. When is the meeting?"

"Today at 2:00 p.m."

"I think you're ready for Round 3."

Susan smiled. For the first time in her career, she felt she was truly making a difference. She felt empowered to do her job and not worry about being slowed down by corporate politics. An opportunity to implement her own strategies in a corporate environment was priceless.

"This is called strategic planning, Susan. Once your strategies are in place, you will have built the foundation for tactical planning and implementation. Good luck this afternoon."

CHAPTER 10

Joshua was upset. He had every intention of firing Greg. It was because of him that Joshua was almost fired. Joshua could not tolerate this type of behavior. He intended to set an example with Greg so this wouldn't happen again. Just as he picked up the phone to call Greg to his office, it rang. It was Susan.

"Hi, Susan."

"Hello, Joshua. Do you have a second? I wanted to tell you all about the big meeting I just had with all the big guns."

What the hell. I would rather hear what happened with Susan's big meeting than deal with Greg. I will deal with him later, Joshua thought to himself.

"Sure. I'll be right there."

****

"So how did it go?" Joshua asked as he entered Susan's office.

Susan smiled.

"Congratulations! So they agreed just like that?" Joshua said with admiration.

"Not just like that," Susan sighed. "Of course Edward played the devil's advocate, but I was ready for every one of his questions because I'd done my research. Research has always been one of my strong suits, but thanks to Kelsey, I've learned to enhance my due diligence, and all of my skill sets. A couple of other concerns cropped up but by the time I minimized their risks of failure, they pretty much just agreed to it."

Just then, Kelsey entered the office.

"Speaking of the devil," Susan chided.

"I heard the good news, congratulations," Kelsey replied.

"No, thank you," Susan returned.

"I've got to get going," Joshua said. "Kelsey, I would like to go over few things with you. Would you mind stopping by when you get a chance."

Even though he had decided on how he was going to handle Greg, Joshua wanted to consult with Kelsey first.

"Will do."

"Susan, congratulations again and we can talk more later. Kelsey, see you soon." Joshua left Susan's office.

"Joshua, I'll be with you after I go over a few things with Susan."

Kelsey sat down.

"So how did it go?"

"Exactly like you said it would. They challenged me on several issues, but fortunately I was prepared for them. I was so thorough, that yes was the only answer left to give by the end of the presentation."

Kelsey nodded in approval.

"Now we need to talk about your next move."

****

Kelsey knocked on Joshua's office door.

"Come in."

"How are you doing?" Kelsey greeted him as he entered.

"Not so good," Joshua replied. "Do you have a second?"

"Sure," Kelsey sat down.

"I'm firing Greg."

"For what?" Kelsey asked.

"I just had the scare of my life. I thought for sure I was about to get fired. Greg sent out a survey form to all our customers without my approval, and wouldn't you know it, some of them called Konrad and complained. That's unacceptable."

"In some circles, yes, but let me ask you, whose fault is it?"

"What do you mean?"

"Did you make it clear to him not to send the survey without your approval?"

Joshua paused. That was not the response he expected, but somehow he still wasn't surprised.

"Actually I didn't."

"So was this a failure in leadership or an employee failure? Maybe his motivation was to impress you," Kelsey stated.

"Regardless, he almost cost me my job."

"Let's just sit back and think about this. What are the pros and cons of firing him?"

Joshua sat back and pondered Kelsey's statement.

"How much value does he bring to your division? How quickly can you replace him? How long would it take for you to get his replacement up to speed? Given the current status of the company, is now a good time to be training someone?"

"I didn't think about that," Joshua admitted.

Kelsey continued with clarification and practical reasoning.

"If Greg was a bad apple, vindictive and purposely bringing harm to your department, I'd be the first to say, get rid of him; but if he is a good employee, then it's your job to hold this together. Remember this, corporations and people do not change. You have to make the change and the adjustment to bring it together. How do you do that? By actually caring. Did you think just by giving him a promotion that that would fix everything? No, it's not that easy. You have to actually take the time to get to know your employees and understand them. Establish trust. Let them know it's ok to make a mistake and teach them how to improve upon it.

"I'm going to leave you with a quote from John Travolta and the movie 'Phenomenon.' Don't laugh that I am quoting movies, but I thought this movie was deep. 'Society is so focused on technology, trying to grasp the fundamentals of science, yet we are failing to grasp what's important. What I am talking about is the human spirit. That's the challenge; that's the voyage; that's the expedition.' Do the right thing and don't let your pride or ego get in the way of caring for your people. Good night and I will see you tomorrow."

Joshua sat back as he tried to process what he had just heard. He finally began to see what Susan was talking about and began to trust Kelsey. He just might really know what he is talking about.

Kelsey's Journal: Earning Joshua's respect was not a foregone conclusion. I'm glad we seemed to have turned a corner. Joshua has natural leadership abilities. If he continues on a deliberate path of balance, he will have the power to transform the lives of those who report to him for decades to come.

"Hey, Joshua," Greg said as he entered.

"Hey, Greg. Have a seat."

"What's going on?"

"I was called into the President's office today."

"Is everything ok?"

"He'd gotten several complaints from some of our clients. Apparently they were unhappy with some of the questions that were asked to answer on that survey form."

Greg looked down with disgust.

"He wasn't too happy, and he was even more disappointed that I didn't know the survey form had been sent."

"I'm sorry, man," Greg shook his head. "I was just trying to be proactive. I didn't think it would be that big of a deal."

"Yeah, well, it was."

There was a moment of silence between them.

"So what now?" Greg asked.

"Greg," Joshua began, "I've got to know what is going on! I don't have to have my hand in the middle of it, but I have to know the main things that are going on in our department and keep me in the loop. From now when it comes to major communication, nothing can go out without my approval. Also, keep me updated with things you feel I need to know and we will make adjustments as to what you can handle on your own and what I need to know. I could have been fired. Let me put it to you this way: Before you do something, you need to ask yourself the question. 'Is Joshua going to support me?' If the answer is no or I don't know, then you need to get my input. Going forward, if you chose to do something on your own, be prepared to accept the consequences. With risk comes great reward, but there is also something called calculated risk. I am working *with* you. Use me. You are not a burden. I don't know it all and I don't expect you to either, but I guarantee you two heads are better than one."

"I know. I'm sorry."

"On a brighter side, it wasn't all bad. Konrad read over the survey form and actually liked it. He wants us to continue developing it, and he wants to look it over."

Greg showed the smile of relief.

"Let's make it happen, man."

"Will do."

****

Kelsey sat across from Konrad's desk. It was his final evaluation meeting. He recalled his previous evaluations as an employee, how he had to brace himself to hear his shortcomings over the past year, to find out how small the percentage would be for his raise. This evaluation was different. He would truly be judged on the success of his work and this would determine the status of his future with this company as a consultant.

"Well, Kelsey," Konrad began, "I'll be honest. Our numbers only slightly improved over the last quarter, but that's ok. I didn't expect a significant difference so quickly, but I must admit I'm impressed. I've seen the morale shift in our management staff. They are more energetic and eager to make a difference in the company. I think this is a direct result of your efforts. If you are interested, I'd like for you to stay for another quarter."

"I'd love to, Konrad," Kelsey said, pleased.

"Now let's discuss the challenges ahead," Kelsey said purposefully. "What is the strategic vision for Realty Solutions? How are you going to create a vision statement that forces your employees to remake this company? Leadership is lonely. Finding a good confidant is not easy. As you embark upon this journey, you will probably get pushed back by your staff; Wall Street Analysts; the Board of Directors; and most importantly your Customers. This journey will be draining and you might question yourself what have you got yourself into; but as the CEO of this company, your job is to lead. Learning to replenish yourself throughout this journey is something that I will help you discover.

"Are you ready for the journey?"

Kelsey's Journal: We are at the precipice of meaningful change. But let us not become complacent just because our perspective has changed. The success of Reality Solutions and its employees is inextricably tied to the execution of their shared vision, the foundation of which is Executive Leadership.

"To me the function and duty of a quality human being is the sincere and honest development of one's potential."

— *Bruce Lee*

......to be continued.

ABOUT THE AUTHOR

Anthony Jackson, having served in the United States military and "Corporate America" for over 20 years, now focuses on helping organizations migrate to a "Green Technology" platform by helping with strategy development through an executive leadership platform. He works on the East Coast with an IT Systems Integrator. He is also President and Co-Founder of Southern Shaolin Academy, a Kung-Fu School located in Ewing, NJ, where he practices and teaches Tai Chi. (More information can be found at www.daoconcepts.com.)

Jackson received his B.S. in Mechanical Engineering (Energy Systems) from the United States Military Academy, West Point, New York, and has also completed various Executive Leadership Development Courses which include the course sponsored by the London Business School. As an Officer in the United States Army, Tony served as an Airborne Ranger Infantryman with distinction while deployed to the first Gulf War; the Somalia Conflict; Honduras; Panama; Egypt; and Israel. Jackson received numerous awards and citations while attached to the 10th Mountain Division.

Jackson's professional career has led him to work at several prominent organizations including his last assignment as the Vice-President of Branded Pharmaceuticals at AmerisourceBergen where he managed over 40 Billion dollars in contracted spending. AmerisourceBergen, NYSE: ABC is currently ranked 22 on the Fortune 500 business list. His other assignments also included: Nestle Beverage Company;

The Dial Corporation; Givaudan Roure; & Roche Pharmaceuticals. Jackson also owned a software development company, specializing in inventory management, before the software was acquired by LMC.

Jackson is currently on the Supply Chain Management Steering Committee at Rutgers University, helping to bring the best in-class business practices to the students, faculty, & business sponsors of Rutgers' Supply-Chain Academic Programs. He has also spoken at numerous industry-related forums and engages in motivational speaking opportunities.